Welcome to Pemfort

Sarah Power

methuen | drama
LONDON • NEW YORK • OXFORD • NEW DELHI • SYDNEY

METHUEN DRAMA
Bloomsbury Publishing Plc, 50 Bedford Square, London, WC1B 3DP, UK
Bloomsbury Publishing Inc, 1359 Broadway, New York, NY 10018, USA
Bloomsbury Publishing Ireland, 29 Earlsfort Terrace, Dublin 2, D02 AY28, Ireland

BLOOMSBURY, METHUEN DRAMA and the Methuen Drama logo are trademarks of Bloomsbury Publishing Plc.

First published in Great Britain 2026

Copyright © Sarah Power, 2026

Sarah Power has asserted their right under the Copyright, Designs and Patents Act, 1988, to be identified as Author of this work.

Photography by MOJA.WTF

All rights reserved. No part of this publication may be: i) reproduced or transmitted in any form, electronic or mechanical, including photocopying, recording or by means of any information storage or retrieval system without prior permission in writing from the publishers; or ii) used or reproduced in any way for the training, development or operation of artificial intelligence (AI) technologies, including generative AI technologies. The rights holders expressly reserve this publication from the text and data mining exception as per Article 4(3) of the Digital Single Market Directive (EU) 2019/790.

Bloomsbury Publishing Plc does not have any control over, or responsibility for, any third-party websites referred to or in this book. All internet addresses given in this book were correct at the time of going to press. The author and publisher regret any inconvenience caused if addresses have changed or sites have ceased to exist, but can accept no responsibility for any such changes.

No rights in incidental music or songs contained in the work are hereby granted and performance rights for any performance/presentation whatsoever must be obtained from the respective copyright owners.

All rights whatsoever in this play are strictly reserved and application for performance etc. should be made before rehearsals begin to Independent Talent Group, 40 Whitfield Street, London, W1T 2RH. No performance may be given unless a licence has been obtained.

A catalogue record for this book is available from the British Library.

Library of Congress Control Number: 2026934222

ISBN: PB: 978-1-3506-4359-8
ePDF: 978-1-3506-4360-4
eBook: 978-1-3506-4361-1

Series: Modern Plays

Typeset by Mark Heslington Ltd, Scarborough, North Yorkshire

For product safety related questions contact productsafety@bloomsbury.com.

To find out more about our authors and books visit www.bloomsbury.com and sign up for our newsletters.

About Soho Theatre

Soho Theatre is London's most vibrant producer of new theatre, comedy and cabaret. A charity and social enterprise, we're driven by a passion for working with bold stories and distinctive artists, connecting them with audiences in original style and creating memorable nights out.

From our early roots in the radical 1970s Soho Poly, we've grown – *and grown* – from a tiny fringe space into a widely influential cultural organisation operating across our four London performance spaces; through international touring and collaborations with India and elsewhere; as festival regulars from Edinburgh Festival Fringe to Melbourne International Comedy Festival; and filming shows and creating our own digital work seen across social platforms and inflight.

Alongside working with some of the most exciting theatre-makers and comedians in the world, we also nurture the next generation of artists through a thriving range of artist and talent development programmes, artists under commission and in development, and two new writing awards including UK's longest established playwriting prize, the Verity Bargate Award.

In 2025 we celebrated 25 years at our central London venue Soho Theatre – described by Phoebe Waller-Bridge as the 'the mothership of new artists', Ryan Calais Cameron as 'a major launchpad' and Bryony Kimmings as 'an extraordinary place for people whose work is genre pushing' – whilst opening London's newest venue, the 'jaw-dropping 1000 seat new theatre' (Time Out), Soho Theatre Walthamstow in May 2025.

sohotheatre.com | @sohotheatre | @sohotheatreindia

Soho Theatre Staff

EXECUTIVE and SENIOR TEAM

CEO & Executive Director Mark Godfrey **Co-Executive Director** Sam Hansford **Co- Creative Directors** Rose Abderabbani (Theatre Programme), Steve Lock (Comedy), Jessica Draper (Creative Engagement) **Operations Director** Edel McGrath **Co- Audience & Communications Directors** Peter Flynn, Kelly Fogarty **Fundraising and Partnerships Director** Bhavita Bhatt **Head of Food & Beverage** Scott Viney

TRUSTEES

Chair Dame Heather Rabbatts DBE **Board Members** Nicholas Allott OBE, David Aukin, Farzana Baduel, Lucy Davies, Martin Esom, Hani Farsi, Campbell Glennie, Lornette Harley, Fawn James, Shaparak Khorsandi, Kate Mayne, David Reitman

TEAMS

Executive Assistant Annie Jones **Theatre** Eve Allin, Alessandro Babalola, Max Elton, Pooja Sivaraman, Paul Sirett, Maddie Wilson, Daljinder Johal, Ellen Ritchie **Comedy** Kathryn Craigmyle, Lee Griffiths, Jet Vevers, Lola Ferguson, Eilis Woods **Creative Engagement** Jenny Bakst, Jules Haworth, Shazad Khalid, Déviniat Adedibu **Press & PR** Augustin Wecxsteen (Campaign Lead), Ruby Willis, Lou Doyle **Marketing** Kia Noakes (Campaign Lead), Val Londono, Alicia Bridge, Flo Granger **Graphic Design** Conor Jatter, Ludmila Bogatchek **Digital** Rhys Matthews, Laura-Inès Wilson, Jody Davies **Audience & Sales** Mariko Primarolo, Jack Cook, Fuad Ahammed, Lainey Alexander, Kitty Smith, Luke Talboys, Sophie Greaves, Sami Sumaria, Erin Handford, Catriona Davidson, Joel Lockhart **Operations** Paul Symes, Gianna Schuetz-McKinnis, Laura Schofield, Em Carr, Dee Lindo, Louisa Pennell, Luca Newman **Technical** Stefan Andrews, Rob

Johnson, Ben Goodwin, Tom Younger, Lydia Edwards, Charlie Leslie, Yas Trowbridge, Aidan Walker, Zac Brewin, Finley Dickins **Food & Beverage** Rishay Naidoo, Ronnie Matczuk, Damian Regan, Evan Jones, Nes Dyer, Abin Marson, Cazz Regan, MD Ridoy Khan, Lisa Gilroy, Georgia Pierce

Audience Team Soho Mischa Alexander, Erol Arguden, Brenton Arrendell, Farah Ashraf, Aiyana Bartlett, Ellie Bibby, Iona Brown, Auriella Campolina, Becca Carr, Geri Carr, Lanre Danmola, Anais Dos Santos, Bronya Doyle, Ben Fallaci, Gabriel Harris, Oscar Holloway, Andrew Houghton, Hana Jennings, Lee King-Brown, Mariama Mansary, Tilly Marples, Faith Martin, India Martin, Kit Miles, Eve Millward, Benji Morris, Paul Murphy, Fiona Oakley, Jack Parry, Janisha Perera, Jesse Phillippi, Rosie Revan, Alexis Sakellaris, Genevieve Sabherwal, Genevieve Sinha, Johnie Spillane, Dylan Sweet, Abby Timms, Lauren Tranter, Jade Warner-Clayton, Joanne Williams, Arthur Yang

Technical Team Soho Liz Barker, Bryn Jones, Jordan Lewis, Florian Lim, Jem Rohde, Abbie Sage, Han Sayles, Maddie Whiffin

Soho Theatre Bar Sneha Adhikari, Anand Choudhary, Mike Giraldo Cifuentes, Sofia Dixon, Lauryn Giovanni, Bibin Gopi, Madeleine Hilton, Dizolele Isaac, Zara Mehrban, Tayafur Rahman, Fatemeh Sarebannejad, Anandhu Sudhakaran, Sian Walsh, Chi Whon Won, Zaza Wright

Soho Theatre Supporters

Principal Supporters
Hedley and Fiona Goldberg
Michael and Isobel Holland
Linda Keenan
Soho Circle

Supporting Partners
Matthew Bunting
Stephen Garrett

Angela Hyde-Courtney
Phil & Jane Radcliff
Jonathan Rees

Corporate Sponsors
Adnams Southwold
Bargate Murray
Character Seven
Financial Express
NBC Universal International Studios
Soho Estates

Trusts & Foundations
The 29th May 1961 Charitable Trust
The Andor Charitable Trust
Bloomberg Philanthropies
Bruce Wake Charitable Trust
The Boris Karloff Charitable Foundation
The Boshier-Hinton Foundation
Chapman Charitable Trust
The Charlotte Bonham-Carter Charitable Trust
The D'Oyly Carte Charitable Trust
Dominic Webber Trust – Core Values
The Fenton Arts Trust
Fidelio Charitable Trust
Garrick Charitable Trust
The Goldsmiths' Company
Harold Hyam Wingate Foundation
Hyde Park Place Estate Charity
The Ian Mactaggart Trust
The Idlewild Trust
The John Thaw Foundation
John Lyon's Charity
KKL Charity
The Kobler Trust
Lara Atkin Charitable Foundation
The Leche Trust
The Mackintosh Foundation
Mohamed S. Farsi Foundation

#My Westminster Fund
Noel Coward Foundation
The Peggy Ramsay Foundation
The Rose Foundation
The Royal Victoria Hall Foundation
Santander Foundation
Schroder Charity Trust
The St James's Piccadilly Charity
Tallow Chandlers Benevolent Fund
The Teale Charitable Trust
The Thistle Trust
Unity Theatre Charitable Trust

Soho Theatre Performance Friends
Ali Braithwaite
Anna Bordon
Amanda Rajkumar
Helen Evans
Bhags Sharma
Rich Thorpe
Chris Thomas
Gary Wilder

Soho Theatre Playwright Friends
Maital Dar
Mrs Emily Fletcher
Liam Goddard
Andrew Lucas
Emma Whitting

Cast

Kurtis – Sean Delaney

Uma – Debra Gillett

Glenn – Ali Hadji-Heshmati

Ria – Lydia Larson

Creative Team

Writer – Sarah Power

Director – Ed Madden

Set and Costume Designer – Alys Whitehead

Associate Set and Costume Designer – Victoria Maytom

Lighting Designer – Cheng Keng

Sound Designer and Composer – Max Pappenheim

Casting Director – Becky Paris

Production Manager – Tom Davis-Coleman for The Production Family

Costume Supervisor – Florence McGlynn

Props Supervisor – Anna Hunt

Tapestry Design – Ellie Foreman-Peck

Intimacy Director – Georgina Makhubele

Fight Director – Enric Ortuño

Wellbeing Support – Tricia Gannon for Artist Wellbeing Company

Company Stage Manager – Lisa Cochrane

Deputy Stage Manager – Abi Morris

Assistant Stage Manager – Charlotte Smith-Barker

Theatre Producer for Soho Theatre – Eve Allin

Production Assistant for Soho Theatre – Daljinder Johal

Executive Producer for Soho Theatre – David Luff

CAST

SEAN DELANEY – Kurtis

Sean is soon to star in the anticipated A24 series *It Gets Worse*, created by and starring Leo Reich. He is best known for his regular role in *Killing Eve*, written by Phoebe Waller-Bridge and directed by Harry Bradbeer. He played the leading role of Teddy in the BBC/AMC series *Life After Life*, directed by John Crowley, based on the book by Kate Atkinson. His other screen credits include *Venom: Let There Be Carnage*, where he played a young Stephen Graham, directed by Andy Serkis.

Sean's theatre credits include the Tony-/Olivier-winning Jez Butterworth play *The Ferryman* (West End and Broadway); *The Vortex* (dir. Daniel Raggett, Chichester); *Brilliant Jerks* (Southwark Playhouse); and Beth Steel's *Labyrinth* (Hampstead Theatre).

He trained at RADA.

DEBRA GILLETT – Uma

Debra Gillett is an actress with an extensive career across theatre, film, television, and radio.

Recent stage credits include *Welcome to Pemfort* and *Pandemonium* (Soho Theatre); *Exit the King*, *Young Chekhov: The Seagull*, *Young Chekhov: Ivanov*, *Three Days in the Country*, *A Small Family Business* and *Tartuffe* (National Theatre); *Noises Off* (Lyric Hammersmith); *The Madness of King George III* (Nottingham Playhouse); and *Limehouse* (Donmar Warehouse). She was nominated for an Olivier Award for Best Comedy Performance for *The Country Wife* by the Royal Shakespeare Company.

Film credits include: *The Critic* (dir. Anand Tucker); *Bridget Jones's Baby* (dir. Sharon Maguire); *Pride and Prejudice and Zombies* (dir. Burr Steers) and *Notes on a Scandal* (dir. Richard Eyre).

Television credits include: *Inside No. 9* (BBC); *Call the Midwife* series 3 (BBC); *Cranford Chronicles* (BBC Television); and *Doctor Who* (DW Productions/BBC Television).

Radio credits include: *Loot* (BBC Radio); *Little Animal Ark Stories* and *Indigo Star* (Heavy Ent Ltd.)

ALI HADJI-HESHMATI – Glenn

On stage, Ali recently played the major role of Simon in *Lord of the Flies* at The Chichester Festival Theatre and played in the four-hander *Antigone (On Strike)* at the Park Theatre. On screen, he was a series lead in *Lockwood & Co.* created by Joe Cornish for Netflix. Alongside this, he had a regular role in the comedy *Bad Education* for the BBC, directed and written by Jack Whitehall and Freddie Syborn. Prior to this, Ali was seen as the large recurring role of Abs Shah in the final series of *Holby City* and can also be seen in the role of Javid in *Alex Rider* for Sony Pictures Television and Amazon Studios.

LYDIA LARSON – Ria

Lydia is an actor and writer from the West Midlands. She performed her debut play *Finding Fassbender* at Pleasance, Edinburgh Fringe and Vault Festival and it received its American premiere at Inis Nua Theatre, Philadelphia.

Other theatre credits include: *The Good John Proctor* (Jermyn Street); *You Stupid Darkness* (Paines Plough); *Skin a Cat* (Offie Shortlisted Best Actress; Bunker Theatre and tour); *Brutal Cessation*, *Travesty* (Assembly Rooms); *We Have Fallen* (Underbelly); *The After-Dinner Joke*, *Springs Eternal* (Orange Tree); *Persuasion* (Salisbury Playhouse); *24 Hour Plays* (Old Vic); *Pride and Prejudice* (Theatre Royal Bath and Number One tour); *Arcadia* (Sonia Friedman Productions).

TV and film credits include: *The Syndicate* (Halcyons Heart Films/Channel Four); *Safari* (My Accomplice); *Wool Coat* (Purl Works); *Father Brown*, *Call the Midwife*, *Doctors* (BBC); *A Gift from Bob* (Studio Pictures).

CREATIVES

Writer – Sarah Power

Sarah's play *Grud* was produced at Hampstead Theatre in 2024 and was nominated for an Off-West End Award for Best New Play. She has recently been on attachment at the National Theatre and has an original TV project in development with Pulse Films.

Director – Ed Madden

Ed has directed the world premieres of *The Habits* and *Octopolis* (Hampstead Theatre); *This Might Not Be It* (Bush Theatre); *Yellowfin* (Southwark Playhouse); *A Table Tennis Play*, and *Lemons Lemons Lemons Lemons Lemons* (Walrus). In dance and opera, he has directed *Così fan tutte* (Da Ponte Festival); *The Limit* (Royal Ballet); and *The World's Wife* (Welsh National Opera). He is from Bristol and based in London, where he is Associate Dramaturg at the National Theatre.

Set and Costume Designer – Alys Whitehead

Alys Whitehead is a set and costume designer who trained at Central Saint Martins. She was a resident designer at the New Diorama Broadgate studios and was a 2024 JMK finalist.

Designer credits include: *Dido and Aeneas* (Longborough Festival Opera); *Gullivers Reisen* (Co-Costume Designer with Rosanna Vize, Deutsches Nationaltheater and Staatskapelle Weimar); *Revenge: After the Levoyah* (Yard Theatre, Soho Theatre); *The Da Vinci Code* (Salisbury Playhouse, Mercury Theatre Colchester); *The Habits* (Hampstead Theatre); *Tender* and *This Might Not Be It* (Bush Theatre); *Bedroom Farce* (Queen's Theatre Hornchurch); *The Angry Brigade* (LAMDA); *Sorry We Didn't Die at Sea* (Park Theatre); *Snowflakes* (Park Theatre); *Lysistrata* (Lyric Hammersmith); *Sad* (Omnibus); *Maddie* (Arcola Theatre).

Associate Designer credits include: *Macbeth* (Pinter); *The Glass Menagerie* (Rose Theatre, Belgrade Theatre, Alexandra Palace and UK tour); *Earthworks* (Young Vic); *Wordplay* (Royal Court).

Associate Set and Costume Designer – Victoria Maytom

Victoria is a designer working across theatre and exhibition design.

She trained at Rose Bruford and was shortlisted for the Linbury Prize 2021.

As Set and Costume Designer: *I Know, I Know, I Know* (Southwark Playhouse); *Surfacing* (Vault Festival and UK tour); *I, Lord* (Bloomsbury Theatre); *Play Without a Title* (New Diorama); and *Gut Girls* (Stratford Circus).

As Associate Designer: *The Code* and *Here* (Southwark Playhouse); *The Da Vinci Code* (Salisbury Playhouse); *A Practical Guide . . .* (TARA Theatre); *Handbagged* (UK tour); *House of Flamenka* (Peacock Theatre, Sadlers Wells); and *Rumplestiltskin* (Park Theatre).

Exhibition design: *Trinity Clocktower* (Trinity Theatre Tunbridge Wells).

Lighting Designer – Cheng Keng

Cheng Keng is a scenographer, lighting and video designer based in London. He trained at Royal Central School of Speech and Drama, completing an MFA in Scenography.

Theatre credits include: *Loop* and *Bungalow* (Theatre503); *The Quiz*, *1984*, *Frankenstein* and *Rain Weaver* (Cockpit); *Poetess* (Jack Dome); *Testament*, *555*: *Verlaine en Prison* and *Double Bill: At the Statue of Venus and La Voix Humaine* (Arcola); *Riders to the Sea* (MAST); *The Light Princess* (The ARC); *Going for Gold* (Park Theatre); *The Lonesome Death of Eng Bunker* and *Tiger* (Omnibus); *Grud* (Hampstead Theatre); *Grills*, *Project Atom Boi* and *So That You May Go*

Beyond the Sea (CPT); *1884* (Shoreditch Town Hall); *The Littlest Yak* (Marlowe Studio); *Chriskirkpatrickmas* (Seven Dials Playhouse); *Let Your Hands Sing in the Silence* (Marlowe Theatre); *these words that'll linger like ghosts till the day i drop down dead* (Pleasance); *The Retreat* and *Pennyroyal* (Finborough); *The Zone* (Taoyuan Art Centre); *Sankofa: Before the Whitewash* (Roundhouse); *Beauty and the 7 Beasts* (Brixton Jamm); *Borders* (Drayton Arms Theatre); *Blue Island 99* (International Dublin Gay Theatre Festival); and *Hello World* (National Taichung Theatre, Taiwan).

Sound Designer and Composer – Max Pappenheim

Theatre credits include: *The Forsyte Saga* (Royal Shakespeare Company; Park Theatre); *Christmas Day* (Almeida Theatre); *Noughts and Crosses* and *Twelfth Night* (Regent's Park Open Air Theatre); *A Raisin in the Sun* (Headlong); *The Night of the Iguana* (Noël Coward Theatre); *The School for Scandal* and *Crooked Dances* (Royal Shakespeare Company); *Cruise* (Apollo Theatre; Duchess Theatre); *Coram Boy* and *Macbeth* (Chichester Festival Theatre); *Shed: Exploded View* (Royal Exchange); A *Doll's House Part 2* and *The Way of the World* (Donmar Warehouse); *Personal Values*, *The Habits*, *The Invention of Love*, *King James*, *Nineteen Gardens*, *Blackout Songs*, *Linck & Mülhahn* and *Labyrinth* (Hampstead Theatre); *The Children* (Manhattan Theatre Club; Royal Court); *Village Idiot* and *One Night in Miami* (Nottingham Playhouse); *Henry V* (Shakespeare's Globe; Headlong); *Hamlet* (Bristol Old Vic); *Ophelias Zimmer* (Schaubühne; Royal Court); *Feeling Afraid as if Something Terrible is Going to Happen* and *Old Bridge* (Bush Theatre); *The Homecoming* and *My Cousin Rachel* (Theatre Royal Bath); *Playhouse Creatures*, *Churchill in Moscow*, *Humble Boy*, *Blue/Heart* and *The Distance* (Orange Tree Theatre); *Single White Female* (national tour); *The Talented Mr Ripley* (national tour); *Picture You Dead* (national tour); *Art* (national tour); *The Syndicate* (national tour); *Murder in the Dark* (national tour); *The Mirror Crack'd* (national tour); *Wish You*

Were Dead (national tour); *The Circle* (national tour); *Looking Good Dead* (national tour).

Opera and Ballet credits include: *Kirsten Flagstad* (Bergen International Festival); *The Limit* (Royal Ballet); *The Marriage of Figaro* (Salzburg Festival); *Miranda* (Opéra Comique, Paris); *Scraww* (Trebah Gardens).

Awards include: Off West End Award for Sound Design (*Old Bridge*).

Associate Artist of Orange Tree Theatre, The Faction and Silent Opera.

Casting Director – Becky Paris

Becky is currently Head of Casting at Shakespeare's Globe where she has cast over 50 productions for the Globe Theatre and Sam Wanamaker Playhouse. She is also a freelance Casting Director who has worked on theatre projects for the NT Studios, Almeida Theatre, Headlong, ATG, Park Theatre, Southwark Theatre, Hampstead Theatre, Pentabus, HighTide and Sheffield Theatres, as well as a number of short films.

Recent work for Shakespeare's Globe includes: *Mother Courage and Her Children* (Dir: Elle While), *Pinocchio* (Dir: Sean Holmes), *Deep Azure* (Dir: Tristan Fynn-Aiduenu), *The Tempest* (Dir: Tim Crouch), *A Midsummer Night's Dream* (Dir: Holly Race-Roughan, Headlong co-production/UK tour), *Romeo and Juliet* (Dir: Sean Holmes), *The Crucible* (Dir: Ola Ince), *Troilus & Cressida* (Dir: Owen Horsley), *All's Well That Ends Well* (Dir: Chelsea Walker), *Cymbeline* (Dir: Jennifer Tang), *Three Sisters* (Dir: Caroline Steinbeis), *Antony & Cleopatra* (Dir: Blanche McIntyre), *Princess Essex* (Dir: Robin Belfield), *Ghosts* (Dir: Joe Hill-Gibbins), *Othello* (Dir: Ola Ince) and *The Duchess of Malfi* (Dir: Rachel Bagshaw).

Other theatre includes: *Ragdoll* (Jermyn Street Theatre); *The House Party* (Headlong; UK tour); *A View from the Bridge* (Headlong; UK tour); *A Ghost in Your Ear* and *An*

Interrogation (Hampstead Theatre); *Hir* (Park Theatre); *Brilliant Jerks* (Southwark Playhouse); *Anna X* (VAULT Festival).

Production Manager – Tom Davis-Coleman for The Production Family

The Production Family deliver a variety of theatre, dance and live experiences in the UK and across the globe. Recent credits: Manchester international Festival, Museum of Austerity for English Touring Theatre. Upcoming projects include large-scale immersive touring experiences and 'The Other Place' at the Shed, New York and the spring season at Soho Theatre.

Costume Supervisor – Florence McGlynn

Florence McGlynn trained at The Arts University Bournemouth. Her credits as Costume Supervisor include: *The Tempest* (Shakespeare's Globe); *Mamma Mia* (Novello Theatre); *Apex Predator* (Hampstead Theatre); *The Habits* (Hampstead Theatre); Fundraising Gala Dinners (Shakespeare's Globe).

Assistant Supervisor credits include: *Mazeppa* (Grange Park Opera); *Oliver!* (Chichester Festival Theatre; Delfont Mackintosh); *Hills of California* (Sonia Friedman Productions).

Intimacy Director – Georgina Makhubele

Georgina is a South African Intimacy Director based in London. She completed her training through Moving Body Arts' SAG AFTRA accredited training programme in 2024 and is now part of a global intimacy coordination company, Safe Sets. With a passion for performance that began on stage, Georgina continues to pursue both theatre and screen projects.

Credits include: *Emetophobe* (short film); *Pleasure over Matter* (short film); *Difference of Opinion* (short film); *Amsterdam Narcos* (Sky TV); *Candy* (White Bear Theatre); *That Song, Again* (short film); *Mopsie* (short film); *Bungalow* (Theatre503); *Where You Go, There I Am* (short film); *The Habits* (Hampstead Theatre).

Fight Director – Enric Ortuño

Training: MA in Movement Studies (Royal Central School of Speech and Drama), Certified Stage Combat Instructor (British Academy of Stage & Screen Combat), Certified Intimacy Directory (IDC USA – Intimacy Directors & Coordinators).

Theatre credits include: *Waiting for Godot* (Theatre Royal Haymarket); *Machinal* and *The Birthday Party* (Theatre Royal Bath); *Sleepova* (Bush Theatre); *Boys on the Verge of Tears* and *Pandemonium* (Soho Theatre); *Suckerpunch* (National Theatre); *Double Indemnity* (national tour); *Road* (Northern Stage; Oldham Coliseum); *Lit* (Nottingham Playhouse); *Orphans*, *Outlying Islands*, *The Good John Proctor*, *The Laughing Boy* and *Owners* (Jermyn Street Theatre); *Othello* and *Animal Farm* (National Youth Theatre); *Birdsong* (national tour); *The Weatherman* (Park Theatre).

Company Stage Manager – Lisa Cochrane

Lisa is a freelance Stage Manager based in London. She completed her drama school training in Professional Production Skills at Guildford School of Acting. CSM credits include: *Scenes from Lost Mothers* (Clean Break; UK tour); Waterperry Opera Festival (Waterperry House); *Songs for Nobodies* (Ambassadors Theatre); *Habibti Driver* (Bolton Octagon).

Lisa also works as a DSM on touring productions, and at venues including The Orange Tree, Jermyn Street, Guildford Shakespeare Company, Stephen Joseph Theatre and Theatre Royal Bath. This is Lisa's first production at the Soho Theatre.

Deputy Stage Manager – Abi Morris

Abi trained at Guildford School of Acting in MA Stage and Production Management, and previously graduated from the University of Birmingham with a degree in Drama and Theatre Arts.

Recent productions include: *Cinderella* (Cliffs Pavilion); *Little Brother* (Soho Theatre); *A Role to Die For* (Marylebone Theatre); *Alice in Wonderland* (Marylebone Theatre); *King of Pangea* (King's Head Theatre); *Heaven* (UK tour); *Aitopia* (Young Vic Theatre); *My English Persian Kitchen* (Soho Theatre; Traverse Theatre); *In Two Minds* (Traverse Theatre); *Fun at the Beach Romp-Bomp-A-Lomp!!* (Southwark Playhouse); *Boy Out the City* (UK tour); *Exhibitionists* (King's Head Theatre); *The Good Enough Mums Club* (UK tour); *The Boy Who Sailed the Ocean in an Armchair* (Leicester Curve); *The Girls' Guide to Good Sex* (Old Joint Stock); *The Secret Life of Humans* (English Theatre Frankfurt); *Love and Piss* (Edinburgh Festival Fringe 2022); and *I Don't Know What Else to Say* (Kickback Theatre Company).

Assistant Stage Manager – Charlotte Smith-Barker

Charlotte studied English Literature and film at Aberystwyth University and Malmö University in Sweden.

Dresser credits: *Playhouse Creatures* (Orange Tree Theatre)

ASM credits include: *The Rivals* (Orange Tree Theatre; Theatre Royal Bath; Cambridge Arts Theatre); *Seagull: True Story* (Marylebone Theatre); *Romeo and Juliet* (Theatre Royal Stratford East; Sadler's Wells East); *In Praise of Love* (Orange Tree Theatre); *Canned Goods* (Southwark Playhouse); *My Pet Star* (Marlowe Theatre); *Wish You Were Here* (Gate Theatre); *La Boheme* (Longborough Festival Opera); *Testmatch* (Orange Tree Theatre; Octagon Bolton); *Aladdin* (Hackney Empire);

Brassed Off (Aberystwyth Arts Centre); *You Bury Me* (Bristol Old Vic; Edinburgh Lyceum; Orange Tree Theatre); *One Woman Show* (Ambassadors Theatre); *Mary* (Hampstead Theatre); *Cages* (Riverside Studios); *Roundabout Tour* (Paines Plough); *Clybourne Park* (Park Theatre); *Soho Cinders* (Charing Cross Theatre); *The Sweet Science of Bruising* (Wilton's Music Hall); *The Catherine Tate Show Live* (Wyndham's Theatre).

Executive Producer for Soho Theatre – David Luff

David Luff is an independent theatre producer who works across the subsidised and commercial sectors. He was Producer, Head of Theatre and Creative Director at Soho Theatre from 2012 to 2025. Notable world premiere productions he produced for Soho Theatre include the Olivier Award-winning *Boys on the Verge of Tears* by Sam Grabiner directed by James Macdonald; *My English Persian Kitchen* by Hannah Khalil from an original story by Atoosa Sepehr; *Age Is a Feeling* by Haley McGee directed by Adam Brace; *Typical* by Ryan Calais Cameron; and new shows from Kim Noble and Lucy McCormick. Alongside DryWrite he produced the revivals and world tours of *Fleabag* by Phoebe Waller-Bridge and its New York and West End transfers. With his producing partner Patrick Myles he commissioned and produced the world premiere of *Network* by Lee Hall, directed by Ivo van Hove at the National Theatre before transferring to the Belsaco Theatre on Broadway, winning Olivier and Tony Awards. They subsequently commissioned and produced the world premiere stage adaptation of Stanley Kubrick's *Dr. Stragelove*, adapted by Armando Iannucci and Sean Foley, starring Steve Coogan, playing in the West End and Dublin's Bord Gáis Energy Theatre.

With big big thanks to:

Ed Madden – Thank you for building Pemfort with me. It feels as much yours as it is mine and I've loved every second of working on it together.

Ali Hadji-Heshmati, Debra Gillett, Lydia Larson and Sean Delaney.

Alys Whitehead, Victoria Maytom, Cheng Keng, Max Pappenheim, Tom Davis-Coleman, Florence McGlynn, Becky Paris, Georgina Makhubele, Enric Ortuño, Lisa Cochrane, Abi Morris, Charlotte Smith-Barker, Ellie Foreman-Peck, Anna Hunt.

Eve Allin, Max Elton, Daljinder Johal, Kia Noakes, Rose Abderabbani, David Luff, Stefan Andrews, Mark Godfrey and everyone at Soho.

Jessi Stewart.

Laura Power.

And Team Marie's.

Author's note (and a potential spoiler, just as a heads up)

I believe every one of us has the capacity to do something terrible and every one of us has the capacity for great change. What I worry we aren't so good at is giving people a place to *live as changed.* This play is a play for us, the community, about what our role might be in creating a world with less violence in it.

I still don't totally know what I think about it all, I think writing the play was an attempt to work that out. But I do think, if we want to tackle the darkest problems in our society, it is probably best to approach them with practicality and empathy.

I hope you enjoy your visit to Pemfort. Please don't litter.

Notes on the text

A forward dash (/) indicates when the next line should come in.

Dialogue in [square brackets] is not spoken.

Welcome to Pemfort

Characters

Ria, *female, early 30s*
Uma, *female, early 60s*
Glenn, *male, 16 years old*
Kurtis, *male, early 30s*

Key dates in Pemfort's history

1264	*The Battle of the Bishops*
1604	*The Ghost of Lady Drongall*
1777	*The Scandalous Lord Leevage*
1998	*Death of Sally Edwards*
Present	*Pemfort's first Living History event*

Scene One

Lights up and we are in a castle gift shop.

It's a small, slightly rubbish castle. It has big ambitions of being the next Warwick, but in reality it's quite a way off that.

The shop sells fun castle-based items, local arts and crafts and general things the manager, **Uma**, *thinks are fun.*

Everything has a bit of a DIY feel.

Uma, **Glenn** *and* **Ria** *are having a planning meeting.* **Glenn** *has the community notice board propped up on the counter and is using it as a makeshift whiteboard.*

Glenn I just think it's a bad idea.

Uma It's a fun idea!

Glenn Who would be doing the jousting? Is it like an interactive experience or a watching and learning experience?

Uma Interactive.

Glenn No. It cannot be an interactive jousting experience.

Ria I think normally with brainstorming sessions you just write all the ideas down in a sort of free-flowing non-judgmental manner, Glenn. Then decide if you like them later on.

Glenn *writes 'Jousting' on a piece of paper and puts it on the notice board in a highly judgmental manner.*

Uma Do you really not think we could just write the ideas down on a piece of paper, chicken? And put the board back where it was? It's only there's no yoga on Thursday and I wanted to let people know.

Glenn You did let people know, you said it in the last yoga.

Uma Yes but for new people!

Glenn The last time we had a new person at yoga was three years ago.

And that was Ria's aunt.

Uma Why didn't your aunt come back, poppet? She didn't enjoy it?

Ria She said it made her back feel weird 'like it was all straightened out like a rod'.

Uma And she didn't like that? /

Glenn / Can we remain focused on the planning session please everyone.

Ria Ohhhh I know Glenn! What about creepy Lady Ghosty?

Glenn You mean the Ghost of Lady Drongall.

Ria Yeah! We could get someone down in the dungeon jumping out at people all bloody and screaming 'stabbed in the back at my own wedding!'

Glenn Won't that be scary?

Ria Well yeah.

But like, in a fun way.

Beat.

Glenn I don't know.

Beat.

Uma What kind of activities were you imagining sweetheart?

Glenn Well.

I was thinking we could do an interesting talk on the system of land ownership in the 1200s.

Small pause.

Uma Well that sounds excellent. Let's get that on the board shall we.

Glenn, *buoyed slightly, writes his idea down on the board, along with 'Ghost of LD'.*

Glenn And a *historically accurate* re-enactment of the Battle of the Bishops.

Uma Yes! A fabulous idea!

Glenn *writes 'BOTB' on the board.*

Ria Oh my god also we can do when that Jane Austen couple broke up and she set fire to his carriage whilst he was banging his mistress in it!

Glenn They didn't 'break up', nobody 'broke up' in the 1700s.

Also we can't do that because it's a different century.

Uma Well that doesn't matter does it? I think it would be fun!

Glenn It does matter. You can't just select all the bits you think are most fun and put them together.

It's meant to be an educational step back in time. You can't have everyone thinking the Battle of the Bishops 1264 happened just around the corner from the Scandals of Lord Leevage 1777. Everyone will leave more confused than they arrived.

Uma Ah no, I'm sure it'll be fine. We can just explain it's like taking lots of little steps back to different bits of time.

And then forwards again.

And then back again but taking a slightly bigger or smaller step.

And that's what we could call it!

'Taking big and small steps backwards and forwards in time around the castle'.

Beat.

Glenn That is not a good idea.

Also we're a fort not a castle.

Uma Well it's historically ambiguous isn't it, chicken.

Beat.

Glenn Ok look. We have to stop the meeting now because I need to go and do the gate. But can I just say that this has not gone well. And I think your ideas are very bad. And we have LOTS of work ahead of us.

He gives each of them a stern look. Then he leaves.

Uma (*calling after him, and not at all put out*) Ok, poppet, just give us a shout if you need anything!

Uma *makes to crack on with her day, then stops suddenly.*

Ria *looks at her.*

Uma I have this feeling I was meant to mention something to the both of you, but I can't for the life of me remember what it was.

Scene Two

Uma *enters followed by* **Kurtis***; they have just been on a tour of the grounds.* **Kurtis** *seems a bit anxious.*

Uma And this is the gift shop! Where we make most of our money.

The swords are the biggest sellers.

Beat.

And we also serve chai! That's what that big vat is.

I wanted to do mead! Thought that would be quite fun, but you need a licence, so we're sticking to chai for now.

BUT we should have some mead for the Living Lifetime! So that'll be very exciting!

Glenn *enters to grab something whilst correcting* **Uma**.

Glenn Living History.

Uma Sorry poppet?

Glenn It's Living History. The event. It's a Living History event. Living Lifetime would just be 'living' wouldn't it. You wouldn't need an event for it.

Uma And this is Glenn! Who's with us on the weekends normally, but now it's summer we've got you a bit more haven't we?

Glenn Yes.

Uma But not for much longer! (*To* **Kurtis**.) Glenn is off to do an apprenticeship with the conservation team at the British Museum very soon!

Kurtis Oh wow! Congratulations!

Glenn *is still eyeing* **Kurtis** *suspiciously*.

Glenn Thank you.

Uma Glenn this is Kurtis, who's starting with us today.

Glenn I didn't know someone new was starting.

Uma I know I completely forgot to mention it!

Glenn Right.

Well welcome to Pemfort.

(*With a concerned look at* **Uma**.) If you have any questions, please let *me* know.

Kurtis Cheers, thanks.

Glenn *finds what he was looking for and exits.*

Beat – **Uma** *smiles warmly after* **Glenn** *then turns back to* **Kurtis**.

Uma So! Was there anything else we needed to cover?

Kurtis Oh, yeah, Uma. There was one thing . . .

He briefly looks towards the door, checking **Glenn** *is gone.*

Uma Oh yes?

Kurtis *hesitates.*

Uma What was that, poppet?

Kurtis Well I was just . . .

I was just wondering if the others know about my conviction?

Beat.

Uma Oh. No. No I didn't mention it.

Pause.

But I can, if you'd rather.

Kurtis *looks unsure.*

Uma Well have a think how you want to handle it and let me know.

And listen, I know you had a rough time of it in the last place and small towns can sometimes feel a bit, I don't know, curtain twitchers and all a little small-minded or something. But it's not like that here. People are nice, you know.

Beat – she smiles warmly at him.

Right, I'm going to have to head out for a bit now I'm afraid! Sue in the chip shop has just started doing Deliveroo orders and apparently it's gotten totally out of control, only she can't work out how to turn the system off, so now everyone is just completely *desperate* for fish!

So I'm going to have to rush over there, but you'll be alright in here for a bit won't you? I'm sure Glenn will be back soon.

Or actually, saying that he might be taking his mum to an appointment . . .

She is leaving.

Kurtis Oh! Are you sure? I feel a bit like I don't know what I'm doing actually. Is there not like a bit of training on the vat we could do really quickly / or

Uma / Imposter syndrome!

Don't you be thinking like that Kurtis, you can do it!!

She's off.

Kurtis *looks around at the gift shop.*

Kurtis Fuck.

He stands for a moment.

Then he nervously moves over to the counter.

He stands there for a bit.

He opens the chai, looks inside. He notices something in there; he starts to put his finger into the vat to fish it out.

Ria *enters.*

She clocks him.

Kurtis *removes his finger and peers at it.*

Then he clocks her.

He freezes.

Ria Hello . . .

Kurtis Hello.

They consider each other for a moment.

Then **Kurtis** *realises he's working in the shop.*

Hello!

And welcome to . . . Pemfort Castle . . . Fort?

Beat.

This is chai.

Ria Sorry who are you?

Kurtis Kurtis . . .

Are you not . . .

Ria I'm Ria.

I work here.

Kurtis (*very embarrassed*) Ohhhh.

Sure.

Beat.

Ria Do you also work here?

Kurtis Er, yeah. It's my first day.

Ria Oh. Right.

Well, (*gently mocking him*) 'Welcome to Pemfort-castle-fort.'

Kurtis (*embarrassed*) Thank you.

Ria I didn't know we were getting a new person.

Kurtis Yeah . . . I . . . yeah.

Beat.

Ria Right.

Well look is Uma around?

Kurtis No, she's gone out to do . . .

Ria Something sort of vague and urgent?

Kurtis Yeah.

Ria Yeah.

Kurtis Oh right, does that happen a lot?

Suddenly it tumbles out of him.

Because not gonna lie I've been freaking out a bit that it's going to get crazy in here, and I do not know how to use this vat or help someone with questions about the Tudors or do like anything else this job entails and /

Ria / Oh nooo, oh mate.

She starts to laugh.

No don't you worry, nobody ever comes in.

Kurtis What?

Ria You're looking at maybe three people *absolute* maximum.

Kurtis Really? Uma sort of gave the impression this would be the busiest time.

Ria To be fair, on the days when someone does arrive, it is often around this time.

There's a man called Big Dog Pete, he has a really big dog, he sometimes rocks up about this time and walks his dog around the moat a bit.

He says his dog was a horse in a past life which died in a battle on these grounds, and it needs to pay homage to the place of its death.

It's ridiculous, obviously, but also sometimes genuinely quite moving.

There is a pause as she considers **Kurtis**.

Ria Do you want to see a photo of a really cool deer?

Beat.

It's really cool.

Kurtis Sure.

Ria *gets out her phone and shows* **Kurtis** *a photo of a really cool deer – he's genuinely impressed.*

Kurtis Whoah. That is cool to be fair.

Ria He's good isn't he.

We're sort of mates.

Kurtis Oh right.

Ria Or acquaintances maybe.

I keep seeing him at the end of my garden and I nod at him and he stares back, but in this way that seems to say 'oh yes, it's you'.

Kurtis How do you know it's a male?

Ria *smiles at him – it's warm and friendly even though she thinks this is a very stupid question.*

Ria Cause of the antlers.

Beat – **Kurtis** *looks a bit embarrassed.*

Ria Well anyway, I better get on.

Kurtis You not working in here too?

Ria No, I do like upkeep of the grounds and stuff.

Like fun stuff.

Beat.

Outside.

Beat.

Welcome again and everything.

Kurtis Thanks.

Ria *makes to leave.*

Kurtis Hey and thanks for the deer photo.

Ria *smiles at him – a small moment between them.*

Ria No worries.

She exits.

Scene Three

Ria, **Uma** *and* **Glenn** *once again gathered around the notice board.*

Glenn Why do we have this new guy?

Uma To work in the shop.

Ria I didn't think we were looking for anyone for the shop?

Glenn Also he doesn't seem very good.

Uma He's been here one week, poppet.

Glenn And not a productive one.

I don't like his nervous disposition. It's annoying to me.

Uma Well I did want to talk to you about that actually.

Beat – they are looking at her expectantly.

Now it's nothing to be alarmed about, but I just wanted to mention to you both that a long time ago now – Kurtis spent a bit of time in prison.

And he's been finding it hard to find a place which is tolerant of that, and I think it makes him feel quite anxious, so he just asked me to mention it to the pair of you so it's all out in the open.

Beat.

Glenn Why was he in prison?

Uma Oh . . .

She hesitates.

I don't know if he wanted me to say . . .

Glenn Oh my god why!? Is it bad?

Uma It's just not for me / to . . .

Ria / How do you know him?

Is it from N.A.?

Uma *is getting flustered.*

Uma I obviously can't answer that.

Glenn So it is.

Is it drugs then? Possession or something?

Uma –

Glenn It is.

Uma (*flustered*) But look it was all a very long time ago! He's a different man now.

Glenn Going to prison is quite bad though isn't it. Like you don't go to prison for having a small amount of drugs on you.

He must have been dealing. Or hurt someone.

What if he stabbed someone or beat someone up really badly.

There is a pause. **Glenn** *does not look pleased. We can see* **Ria** *mulling it over.*

Ria (*to* **Uma**) Did / he . . .

Then **Kurtis** *enters.*

Kurtis / Hello . . .!

Uma Oh heyyyy there, Kurtis!

Awkward pause.

Come on in, we were just talking about how nice it is to have you with us.

Another awkward pause.

Kurtis *smiles at* **Ria**.

Kurtis I think I saw that guy with the really big dog go by earlier.

Beat.

He didn't come in though.

Ria Glenn has a theory on that.

Glenn It's not 'a theory', it's true.

(*To* **Kurtis**.) It's because you aren't Uma.

He only comes in if she's in the shop because he fancies her and wants to talk to her. And then he makes up all that stuff about his dog being haunted as an excuse.

Uma Glenn!

Glenn But actually he knows his dog isn't haunted.

Because obviously a dog isn't haunted.

(*To* **Uma**.) He probably just says that because you seem like the sort of person who would like that kind of thing.

Uma I wouldn't think a dog was haunted!

Glenn I know that's what I'm saying, you *seem* like the sort of person who might believe a dog is haunted, but actually you're much more grounded in reality than the impression you initially give off.

Pause.

Uma Such a lot to unpack there, Glenny.

Glenn *cracks on without unpacking any of it.*

Glenn Now. The first thing on the agenda for today is that I have decided to write a very amazing speech, which I'm planning to make at the event, so I need that added to the running order.

Uma A speech!?

Glenn Yes. It's going to be extremely moving and beautiful and make everyone want to donate a lot of money to the Bell Tower restoration fund.

Uma Well that's so exciting – your mum will love that.

Is she coming, poppet?

Glenn (*not happy about it*) Probably.

Pause.

Ria Well maybe I can find her a task to do in the gardens for the day.

Glenn *and* **Ria** *smile at each other – a moment of understanding.*

Glenn Thanks.

Kurtis *nervously attempts a question:*

Kurtis Are we getting a new bell?

Glenn No there was never a bell.

Well. I mean obviously once there was a bell but like in recent times there's never been a bell.

It's the stonework. Lots of it's damaged so we really need to get it repaired, only the stones are these really special type of stone which curve in this very special way.

They actually think the technique is completely unique to Pemfort. So it's really important to restore it correctly, matching the techniques they'd have used at the time.

Only Pemfort isn't really . . . it's not a priority site, so we need to raise the money ourselves. So the Living History event just really needs to be extremely good and successful so that we can do that before it gets any worse.

He looks anxious again.

Because I love the Bell Tower.

A pause.

Ria It's going to be a huge success, Glenn, we'll make sure of it.

Glenn *smiles at her.*

Glenn Anyway. So. The other thing I wished to discuss today is that seeing as we are moving forward with our 'events from all throughout history with no sense of order or logic' idea, we should make a timeline for clarity.

Uma Well maybe that would be a nice activity to assign to Kurtis.

Glenn I don't think so.

Uma But Kurtis doesn't have an activity assigned to him right now, and it might be a nice way for him to learn the history of the castle.

Glenn *gives* **Uma** *a piercing look.* **Uma** *holds* **Glenn***'s eye.*

Kurtis Oh I don't /

Uma / And get him involved in the event a little.

A silent power struggle seems to happen between **Glenn** *and* **Uma**.

Uma *wins.*

Glenn Fine.

Kurtis you can do the timeline.

Kurtis Sorry what exactly /

Glenn / Just make sure it's good ok. I don't want it to look tacky.

Kurtis *is looking panicked.*

Kurtis Er, sorry what / am I . . .

Ria *smiles at him.*

Ria / I can do it with you, don't worry.

Scene Four

Later in the evening. **Kurtis** *sits, not really doing anything, he is very still.*

Uma *enters.*

Uma You ok there, Kurtis?

Kurtis Yeah, yeah good.

Beat.

Sorry. I'll get going.

Uma You don't have to.

Pause.

How's the flat, is it alright?

Kurtis Ah yeah, it's great yeah.

Thanks so much for that.

Uma No worries.

Beat.

I just got a message from my son, he's going to bring his kids to Living History.

Kurtis Ohhh that's great news. That's a big . . .

Uma It's a big moment for us yes.

She smiles at him.

You feeling weird?

Kurtis Yeah.

Really weird.

Uma Listen, I think you're doing great.

Just keep your chin up and crack on hey, it'll get much easier.

Beat.

Kurtis Thanks for letting me be here.

Uma You're very welcome.

Scene Five

Ria *and* **Kurtis** *on stage, next to a huge piece of cardboard – the beginnings of their timeline.*

There is a tiny feeling of excitement in the air at being alone together.

Ria Right.

I guess we just start with a big line?

Kurtis Sounds good.

Ria *hands* **Kurtis** *a pen as she begins to organise the bits they need for the timeline.*

Kurtis *begins to draw.*

There is a slightly awkward pause as they work.

Ria So you're from London huh?

Kurtis Yeah.

Pause.

And you're from round here?

Ria Yeah, like literally round the corner.

I've known Uma since I was a kid.

And she has not changed *at all*. I think she's still wearing the same fleece.

Ria *suddenly notices what* **Kurtis** *has been up to – he's drawn a really really wonky line.*

Ria Wowwww.

She laughs.

That is terrible.

Kurtis What?

Ria *is gently laughing at him.*

Ria Just draw a line.

Like one straight line.

Kurtis I did.

Beat

Ria No you didn't.

Beat – **Kurtis** *steps back for a bit of perspective.*

He laughs, embarrassed.

Kurtis Oh man.

Ria Let's swap, I'll do the outline and you can do 'vibe' for each one.

Kurtis 'Vibe' being like what hats people were wearing, if cars existed, that kind of thing?

Ria Exactly.

There's a bunch of little things there for you to stick on.

She starts to map out the timeline of Pemfort's history. She continues to draw over the next part of the scene.

There is another slightly awkward pause – which she fills:

How you finding Pemfort so far then?

Kurtis I love it. Everyone here is so . . .

Ria Eccentric? /

Kurtis / Keen for interaction.

Ria *laughs.*

Ria Keen for interaction. That's very true.

But it's not too much interaction?

Kurtis Not at all. I'm also quite keen for interaction, so it's nice.

Ria *laughs.*

Ria Have you been to the swimming yet?

Kurtis What's the swimming?

Ria Ah, well if you're keen for interaction it's the place to be.

Every Wednesday at 6pm, down by the river. There's live music, kids screaming, strange snacks you'll be forced to eat. It's great.

Kurtis I'll have to check it out.

Pause – he is keen to keep the chat going:

Hey how are you and your deer getting on?

Ria Yeah good! I think we're proper mates now you know!

Kurtis Oh cool!

Ria Yeah, it is actually so cool.

She has finished drawing the line and now picks up a roll of tape to maybe secure the timeline more. She starts trying to peel some tape off but it's really not moving – over this next chat she's continuing to try but without luck.

At first I thought maybe I was just being hopeful, but he's definitely coming further into the garden when I'm in there now. Only if my aunt's over he doesn't come in at all. So, I think he definitely knows me, so that's quite cool isn't it!?

Kurtis Definitely.

Ria *picks at the tape again and finally a tiny piece of tape peels off but it's in a weird little useless shape and then she's back to where she started. It's super annoying.*

Ria Oh for fuck's sake!

She throws the roll of tape across the shop floor in frustration. It knocks some stuff over.

Beat – then she laughs, embarrassed.

Sorry. That was stupid.

Kurtis *grins.*

Kurtis No stress.

They both move over to clear up the mess together – both aware of being close to each other as they do it.

Then **Kurtis** *picks up the tape and manages to peel it off successfully – he hands it to* **Ria**.

Ria *is embarrassed.*

Ria (*joking*) Humiliating.

Kurtis *grins.*

Kurtis (*weird joke*) Luck of the . . . peel . . .

Ria *looks a bit confused, she laughs slightly.* **Kurtis** *is embarassed.*

He moves back to the images:

Kurtis So, what do I put for present day?

Ria Jeans?

And a computer . . .? and maybe sort of moral panic?

Kurtis *laughs.*

Scene Six

Glenn, **Uma**, **Ria** *and* **Kurtis** *are all gathered in the shop around the notice board. Everyone is quiet, it has a peaceful feel.*

Glenn *aggressively bangs a sword into the notice board.*

Glenn Everyone! Hello! Excuse me!

Beat.

Ria Glenn nobody was talking.

Glenn (*as if* **Ria** *is an idiot*) I'm just beginning the meeting Ria, that's how you begin a meeting.

Beat.

Ok so listen please everyone because the event is getting closer and closer and we still REALLY need to nail down how we're going to do the Battle of the Bishops. There's only four of us and that is not really screaming 'big battle' is it.

Beat.

I saw this *really* good re-enactment of a battle at Warwick Castle once. It started with this talk by a nobleman but then whilst everyone was absorbed and *thinking* that's what it was all about, suddenly you hear this cry behind you and you turn and hundreds of thousands of *millions* of people in these amazing costumes are charging towards you, with shields and swords and you are like 'OH NO A BIG BATTLE IS ABOUT TO HAPPEN THIS IS VERY SCARY BUT ALSO INFORMATIVE'.

Uma I wish we wouldn't always be comparing ourselves to Warwick Castle, we are our *own* castle.

And they have considerably more funding than us.

Glenn I'm just saying.

It was very good.

Kurtis Er, sorry, just for context . . . what happened in our battle exactly?

Pause as **Glenn** *stares at him.*

Glenn Ok wow, I mean, regardless of working here or not you should *really* know about the Battle of the Bishops.

Ria You really shouldn't.

Glenn It's a HUGE battle of cultural significance to this country /

Ria / It's a really niche battle very specific to this castle /

Glenn / Thank you Ria, I will explain.

He takes a dramatic pause.

The year is 1264, and Pemfort is in the hands of Lady Jane de Bisschop, a Dutch noblewoman loyal to Henry III, and her son Frederik.

Lady de Bisschop is an eccentric and free-spirited character, and she runs Pemfort in a way which, for the time, is revolutionary. She is kind to the people of the surrounding lands, and she holds monthly meetings where she asks everyone for suggestions on how things should be run and implements popular ideas.

So everyone is having a super nice time.

But then! A civil war breaks out in England! And Pemfort is attacked! By a crazy *evil* bishop! Who wants to overthrow Lady Jane de Bisschop because of her loyalty to the King!

Kurtis Whoah . . . what!?

Glenn Yeah!

An *actual* bishop (*mimes a big hat*) attacking the *house* of Bisschop.

Kurtis What are the chances!

Glenn They are very low.

Anyway. The evil bishop, he has a *much* stronger army, and the element of surprise and everything on his side.

BUT because all the people of the land love Jane and Frederik so much, they rise up! And they grab their pots and pans and rush to stand united with the Pemfort soldiers!

And Frederik, he takes a sword, and he goes off and finds the evil bishop and he kills him! Even though he is only sixteen years old.

And then Jane and Frederik and the people of Pemfort all live happily together in a beautiful democracy.

He is looking at **Kurtis** *like 'isn't that incredible'.*

Kurtis That's incredible!

Glenn Yeah. It is.

Kurtis We have to do this battle! So cool!

Glenn But how? When we 'do not have the budget of Warwick'.

There is a pause.

Kurtis Well . . . how about we do something similar to the one you saw? And maybe you can tell the story like you just told it there, except you don't say what happens at the end, you just say something like 'it all came down to the final moments between Freddie and the bishop.'

And you think you're at a storytelling event, but then suddenly Freddie and the evil bishop appear!

And a fight ensues! And you think the evil bishop will take it, but then suddenly . . . Freddie has him!

He looks at **Glenn**'*s face, suddenly losing confidence.*

Kurtis Or something like that . . . I dunno, maybe that's a bit too . . .

Beat.

Glenn That is quite a good idea actually.

Kurtis *is delighted.*

Glenn *is thinking hard.*

Glenn I could be Frederik.

Kurtis Yeah!

Glenn (*to* **Kurtis**, *not a question*) And you can be the evil bishop.

Kurtis *looks horrified at the suggestion.*

Kurtis Oh! Oh well I don't / know . . .

Uma *and* **Kurtis** *speaking over each other:*

Uma / Oh yes perfect!!! /

Kurtis / I think actually I'd rather not be the er, / evil bishop . . .

Uma / Well this is all taking shape *beautifully.*

And Sue said she's happy to be the Ghost of Lady Drongall Glenny, so that's good, isn't it?

Glenn Yeah, she's quite scary, so that works well actually.

Beat.

You know this has been a good and productive session, everyone.

Uma, **Ria** *and* **Kurtis** *exchange a little smile at this sign off from* **Glenn**.

Scene Seven

Glenn *and* **Kurtis** *are practising their sword fighting in the shop. They are using wooden swords from the gift shop to practise, but also on stage are some swords which look much more real deal.*

Glenn *is watching a video on his phone and comparing the video to* **Kurtis**.

Kurtis *does his move, he makes a face of real concentration as he does it.*

Kurtis Like that?

Glenn Yeah!

You have to keep practising though, because it needs to look like you aren't concentrating so hard when we do it in the re-enactment.

Because right now you look a bit –

He makes a weird concentrating face – mimicking **Kurtis**.

Kurtis Yeah . . . ok, sure.

Glenn And then once we have it better, we can try with the real ones.

Kurtis Sounds good.

He practises the move again, half to himself, as **Glenn** *watches him for a moment.*

Beat.

Glenn Where did you work before you worked here?

Kurtis In a warehouse. Why?

Glenn Why did you leave?

Kurtis Er . . . the other guys I guess. We didn't get on. Had some trouble.

Glenn Because you were in prison?

Beat.

Kurtis Yeah.

Pause.

Glenn When did you get out of prison?

Kurtis Seven years ago.

But then was on parole for a bit.

Glenn *looks blank.*

Kurtis That's where you're living in the community, but you have a tag on your ankle, and a curfew, and lots of meetings with parole officers, stuff like that.

Glenn So how long since you've been totally finished? With all that stuff.

Kurtis (*working it out as he answers*) Fffffive years.

Glenn And you worked in the warehouse all that time?

Kurtis Nooooo god no. Just worked there for six months. I've had loads of jobs.

Glenn Like what?

Kurtis *laughs.*

Glenn Am I asking too many questions?

Kurtis No, you're good.

Er, well, let me think, I worked in a shoe shop, in a supermarket, in another warehouse, a library /

Glenn / A library!

You don't seem like someone who'd work in a library.

Kurtis *laughs.*

Kurtis What do I seem like I work in?

Pause as **Glenn** *considers this carefully.*

Glenn Maybe a bowling alley.

Can see you as the guy on the door going (*really bored voice*) *'Do you need the barrier up?'*

Kurtis *laughs.*

Kurtis I'll take it.

Beat.

Glenn What do I seem like I work in?

Kurtis A library.

Glenn Good. That's similar to a museum isn't it.

Beat.

Kurtis You excited to start your apprenticeship?

Glenn Yeah. I'm SUPER excited.

I've been practicing LOADS. Going to the archives and stuff.

And I did some digging for buried objects and then pretended they were artifacts and practised how I would carefully restore them.

I did a key ring which says 'Janet's hen do'.

It looks great now, I think Janet would be very pleased.

Kurtis *laughs.*

Beat – **Glenn** *looks nervous thinking about the apprenticeship.*

Glenn I just really want to be good at it.

Kurtis *looks at* **Glenn**.

Kurtis You're going to be brilliant, Glenn. I mean look how much you've taught me since I've been here. You're already an expert.

Glenn *seems genuinely comforted by this – he smiles at* **Kurtis**.

Glenn Thanks.

Beat.

And Uma is going to look after my mum while I'm away, so that's good.

He remembers **Kurtis** *doesn't know about his mum.*

Glenn She's a bit . . . unwell.

Like mentally.

Kurtis Yeah, Uma mentioned actually.

Glenn Just sometimes. Like mostly she's fine. It's just sometimes she gets a bit upset and anxious but its way more . . . like sometimes she can't move or speak . . .

But not always. Sometimes she's totally fine. She used to be fine all the time when I was little. She could even do quite *risky* things. We used to play this game in the Bell Tower where I would jump from that little stone ledge and catch the iron bar and swing back and forth pretending to be the bell. And I've seen parents freak out when their kids have done that, but she was always totally calm about it. She'd stand below and make the noise of the bell in time as I swung.

Only now I know that would really upset her. I think even just being in a narrow space like that would probably be too much . . .

A pause.

Kurtis My mum was a bit similar actually.

Glenn Really?

Kurtis Yeah. She used to get really distressed sometimes . . . smash stuff up . . . go missing.

Beat.

It's stressful.

Glenn Yeah.

A moment of understanding passes between them.

It is.

A pause, then . . .

Ok, do you want to try the whole sequence together?

Just with the wooden ones obviously.

Kurtis Thank god.

Yeah, let's do it.

Scene Eight

Ria *alone in the shop working on the timeline.*

Kurtis *enters – he's a bit stressed.*

Ria (*joking*) Ohhh here he is. Finally decided to show up.

Kurtis Can I just say I'm not enjoying these cows.

Ria Uhuh.

Kurtis Why are they always looking at me?

Ria They look at everyone.

Kurtis *looks at the timeline.*

Kurtis Well, if I do say so myself, this is looking quite good isn't it.

Ria Glenn came by earlier to inspect our progress and he said for four weeks' work he finds it 'disappointing'.

Kurtis Always with the pep talks that guy.

Ria *grins.*

A pause as **Kurtis** *starts to get settled into the room, maybe puts his stuff down, starts looking through what's left to do on the timeline.*

Ria Everyone was singing your praises at swimming last night.

'Oh Kurtis, that young man is a little gem, he helped me with my garden, he carried my shopping home, he got my kid to stop crying, he's the second coming of Jesus Christ'.

(*Joking.*) Was sickening.

Kurtis *looks embarrassed but pleased.*

Kurtis What can I say, they love my urban charm.

Ria You know I think that does actually have something to do with it. It's like because you're from London everyone expects you to be a complete arsehole, so then the minute you open a gate for them they're falling over themselves to say how polite you are.

Kurtis *grins.*

Ria I thought you were going to come anyway? To the swimming.

Kurtis Yeah, I was planning to, but then I went on this walk Uma recommended and I got so lost using her little guide thing that by the time I finally found my way home it was too late.

I think I saw your deer though you know.

Ria Did it have a thing on its antler? Like a silver thing?

Kurtis I don't think so . . .

Ria Not my guy then.

I'm actually . . . I don't know what to do about that actually, it's been stressing me out.

Kurtis What is it?

Ria He's got this thing all wrapped over his antlers. I think it's like wire or something and I can tell it's really irritating him because he keeps going like this:

She bends her head to the side mimicking the deer.

But it doesn't seem to be budging.

I keep thinking if you could just get close enough to him I think you could get it off pretty easily, and I did actually give it a go the other day but it's just quite scary. Like he could really smack you with those antlers. And then I think he sensed my panic and bolted.

Kurtis Well yeah, I mean fair enough – I can't even get near a cow.

Ria I guess.

I just hate watching how stressed he looks.

Beat.

Were you in the woods then? On this walk?

Kurtis Yeah.

Ria Like Blackthorne? Or closer to the river?

Kurtis Ria I have literally no idea.

Ria *laughs.*

Ria Could you not have used your phone? For the directions.

Kurtis Probably. But I'm not good at it. And it's still just a massive screen of green with some random stiles on it. In London we have actual directions like 'turn right onto Queens Road' instead of things like 'when you get to the big tree turn three quarters towards the sun and walk until you see a sheep'.

Ria I did live in London for a while you know, you don't need to 'in London' at me.

Kurtis Did you? You didn't tell me that.

Ria Yeah, when I was younger.

Kurtis Why did you do that? That does not seem like your vibe *at all*.

Ria Wellllll . . .

She's suddenly awkward.

Kurtis Ohhhhh for a guy was it?

Ria Yeahhhh.

Kurtis Ohhhhhh.

Ria Embarrassinggggg.

Kurtis That's not embarrassinggggg.

Ria It is a bit embarrassingggggg.

But I was young and in loveee and he really wanted to go. And everyone's always saying you've got to hate the little town you're from and want to escape to the big city asap aren't they, so I was like, 'oh right, fuck, I better want to do that too then, off I bloody go!'

Kurtis *laughs.*

Kurtis And you didn't love it?

Ria I didn't hate it. Met some nice enough people. Ate some really nice bao buns, think about those quite a lot actually.

But the whole time I was just thinking 'I wish I was alone in a field right now'.

And then eventually it dawned on me that nobody actually cares what I'm doing with my life except me, so I thought 'oh brilliant, I'll just go back then, that'll be much nicer'.

You can just be a young person who wants to live in the countryside and work in a castle and that is a totally valid use of a life too.

Kurtis *laughs.*

Ria I just wish it hadn't taken me so long to realise that, instead of wasting so much of my twenties . . . stuck.

Beat – suddenly realising who she's talking to.

Sorry, maybe that was a dumb thing to say.

Kurtis Nah not at all, quite comforting to hear to be honest.

And at least you've worked it out now.

I often feel like my whole life I've just been trying to sort out these like basic things like 'ok where am I sleeping, how am I getting some work'. And sometimes I worry if one day I do finally get into a position where I can decide what to do with my time, I have no idea what I would even pick to do.

Do I like looking at tiny insects? Or dressing up as figures from history? Or making jam? I don't know.

Pause as **Ria** *considers this.*

Ria Well what did you like in school?

Kurtis Yeah, I did not really go there.

Ria Ohhhh I see.

Kurtis What did you like in school?

Ria Biology and nature stuff. Obviously.

Kurtis Obviously.

Ria But really that was probably just because of my aunt who's obsessed with it.

So I dunno, I don't even know if it was me picking it really, we're all just products of our environments anyway.

Maybe if I'd grown up in a city, I'd really love . . . performance art.

Kurtis That was my experience of growing up in a city.

CONSTANT performance art.

You couldn't MOVE for performance art, you'd be walking along just trying get to school or down the road to Tesco when suddenly you've found yourself in yet another piece of performance art.

Ria Just as I suspected.

They smile at each other.

Then a pause – she's slightly nervous to ask this:

What about in prison? How did you spend your time in there?

Kurtis Doing a *tonne* of therapy.

Ria Really!?

Kurtis Yeah. With Kev. He was my therapist. Miss that guy.

But did other sessions too. The ward I was on, they were this specialist centre and they had a huge emphasis on mental health, so I got a lot of stuff. CBT, group sessions, art therapy.

Was lucky to get that. It helped a lot to be honest.

Ria Almost good you went hey.

Kurtis *does not respond to this – we sense he disagrees and so does* **Ria**. *It's awkward – she tries to move them on quickly.*

Ria I was thinking . . . we could go swimming at the river this evening? If you're about.

Beat.

You know, seeing as you missed it the other day.

Kurtis Oh yeah great, I thought it was only on Wednesdays.

Beat.

Ria Oh yeah no, it is.

I was thinking like just we could go.

Beat.

Only if you wanted, no worries if you're /

Kurtis / Oh! Yeah no, yeah!

I'd love that.

An excited moment between them.

Kurtis Won't get lost that way either, what with your expert survivalist skills on hand to guide me.

(*Pretending to be* **Ria** *as a survivalist.*) Kurtis come quick! You see these tracks!? Judging from these I think a duck has been here sometime in the last two hours. We must be close to water!

Ria *laughs.*

Ria Uhuh. But you won't be listening because you'll just be next to me panicking all like 'But did I even want to go swimming? Would I have ever picked it if left to my own devices? Who am I!? Ahhhh'.

Kurtis Wowwwwwwwww SAVAGE attack from Bear Grylls.

Ria *momentarily panics.*

Ria Sorry, maybe that was a bit much actually . . . ahh, I feel like I'm saying everything wrong.

Kurtis Nooo not at all, I love it.

They smile at each other.

A pause.

And then, quite naturally and smoothly – **Ria** *kisses* **Kurtis**.

He's surprised, and then he kisses her back.

They break away from each other.

An excited beat. Then . . .

Kurtis Well that was the best thing that's ever happened to me.

Ria *laughs.*

Ria Cringeeee.

But I / love it.

And then we realise **Uma** *is there, she's seen the kiss.*

Uma / Hello.

They both jump.

Ria Oh my god! Uma, you scared me.

Uma *moves more into the room, attempting to seem breezy.*

Uma Well this is coming on nicely.

Kurtis *suddenly seems keen to leave – he starts to get up, get his things together.*

Kurtis Well anyway, I better go . . .

Ria Really? We've barely started.

Kurtis Yeah, sorry, just realised I totally spaced on a chat with Glenn.

He starts to go.

Ria Oh . . . ok . . . well I'll message you about later.

Kurtis *avoids looking at either of them, he's suddenly very awkward.*

Kurtis Yeah, sounds good.

He leaves.

There is a small pause.

Uma What's happening later?

Ria Going swimming.

Uma Oh right.

(*Not convincing.*) Great.

Pause.

Uma You and Kurtis getting on well then?

Ria Yeah.

Uma (*unconvincing*) Great.

Pause – **Ria** *senses* **Uma***'s unease.*

Ria Why are you being weird?

Uma Nothing. That's great.

A pause.

That's great.

Scene Nine

Kurtis *and* **Uma** *alone in the shop.* **Kurtis** *is holding a piece of paper.*

It feels still. Sombre.

There is a pause. Then . . .

Kurtis I think I have to tell Ria.

Beat – they look at each other.

Uma Yes . . . I think so.

Beat.

Or you could just keep it as a professional relationship.

Kurtis I don't want to keep it as a professional relationship.

Uma I know but . . .

Pause.

Kurtis Do you regret offering me the job?

Beat.

Uma (*not totally convincing*) No.

There is a long pause – both of them partly lost in thought.

Uma They think it's to do with drugs.

Kurtis Do they?

Uma Because we know each other from N.A. They just assumed . . . so I just sort of let them . . .

Beat as **Kurtis** *takes this in.*

Kurtis Right.

Fuck.

Beat – he is getting a bit upset.

I wrote out how I would tell her.

Can I read it to you?

Uma *softens.*

Uma Yes.

Of course.

Kurtis *looks at the paper.*

Kurtis Christ.

Beat – **Uma** *doesn't say anything.*

Kurtis *gets himself together a bit.*

Kurtis Ok.

A long pause – then he reads:

Ria. I really like you.

A lot.

Beat.

I feel like we are getting to know each other in a way that feels more personal than it did before, and with that in mind and because I really want that to continue, I need to tell you something about myself.

I am telling you in the hope that maybe, by being totally honest, there is a chance you might be able to continue spending time with me in the way we have been.

I know that isn't likely.

I know that it will probably mean you don't want to keep spending time with me. And I will understand that.

Beat.

When I was younger, I was a very troubled person. My father was a very abusive man, and my mother was battling severe addiction issues. Neither of them had the capabilities to raise a child.

When I was nineteen, I was extremely angry, and I also thought that violence was a completely normal part of life.

I had suffered a lot of neglect and so a lot of the basic lessons about how to be a person that you might have learnt growing up, I hadn't learnt. I didn't understand how to form friendships or relationships. I didn't understand how to sympathise with the position of others properly.

I thought a lot of very disordered things, which it feels very confusing to me now that I ever thought.

But when I was nineteen, I did.

I really need you to know that I don't think those things anymore, I have been through a lot of treatment, and I can confidently and resolutely say that I am not that version of myself anymore. I am the person who is here now, the person you know.

Beat.

But that version of me. Did a really awful thing.

I had been dating a girl, who had started sleeping with somebody else, and I was very upset and angry about that. And one night at a party, when everyone had been drinking, she had started laughing at me in front of all these people.

Not that this is any justification, nothing is justification, but just so you can understand that suddenly, in that moment, all this rage at everything which had happened to me before, and the humiliation and anger at what was happening to me then, it all sort of came together in this one horrendous and unforgiveable act.

Beat.

The charge I was convicted for was aggravated rape. Twelve years ago.

That's why I was in prison.

Beat.

And it feels like this completely other person did that.

But I know that it is what *I* did.

For the rest of my life that will have been what I did.

Beat.

And I hate my past self so much for it. And the way you feel horrified by him and sickened by him and scared of him.

That's how I feel about him too.

And I want more than anything for you to understand that version of me is gone, and a very different me is here now. And I have such huge and overwhelming shame for what I did.

But it's something that you should know.

There is a long pause.

Uma Yes.

Yes, I think that's good.

Scene Ten

Glenn *alone in the shop looking through stuff, clearly looking for something.*

Glenn UMA!

He waits – no response.

He continues looking.

RIA!

He pauses – no response.

He continues looking.

UMA!

Kurtis *enters.*

Kurtis What you looking for?

Glenn The key for the shed. It's meant to be on the hook but it's not there.

A beat – **Kurtis** *looks blank.*

Glenn It's got a goblin on it.

Kurtis Oh . . . I think it's in the fish drawer . . .

Top right fish.

Glenn *moves over and checks the drawer – he finds the key.*

He looks at it and then looks at **Kurtis**, *shocked by what's just happened.*

Glenn Whoah.

Ria *enters.*

Ria Ugh, was very aggy in Co-op.

Kurtis Aggy? Ria there is only ever one person in there slowly buying a sandwich.

Ria Which was too many.

I like an empty shopping experience.

Ria *and* **Kurtis** *smile at each other. It feels flirty somehow.*

Glenn *considers them, unimpressed.*

Glenn Ok. Can you please remember to also work on your timeline whilst you're doing (*gesturing*) this.

Then he exits.

Slightly embarrassed but cute moment between **Kurtis** *and* **Ria**.

Ria Ok, guess we better . . .

A pause as they get out the timeline stuff and begin working.

Kurtis Hey . . . I wanted to ask, is your deer still in a mess with his antler?

Ria Yeah.

Kurtis Cause I was . . . I had an idea of something you could try.

Ria Oh yeah? You going to tell me to start chanting 'you are a confident deer approacher' in the mirror every morning?

Kurtis Oh you know it already huh.

Ria *laughs* – **Kurtis** *grins.*

Kurtis No it's this . . . it's this breathing technique for slowing your heart rate down. It's a bit 'meditation' or whatever, but it is . . . it is actually quite good.

Ria Go on.

Kurtis Ok. Well basically, it's really simple, you just breathe in time with your movement and you keep your movement *really* slow. So I was thinking it might be good as you're approaching him – each step is an inhale or exhale – and you go super slow like . . .

He demonstrates.

And then as you're doing that the idea is you try really hard to just focus on things which are happening in that moment. So you don't let yourself think 'oh man what if he kicks or bolts' or whatever, instead you just focus on thinking 'I am taking one step forward', 'I can feel a breeze on my face' that kind of thing.

He's losing confidence a bit.

It sounds dumb but it does actually . . . It can be quite . . . er . . . helpful.

Ria *is smiling at him.*

Ria Nah it sounds great.

I'll try it for sure.

Kurtis Um, and then also on a more sort of practical level I actually . . . I got you something which might help . . .

Just wait there one sec.

He disappears, there is a bit of noise from off stage.

Then he reappears holding a helmet – but it's been decorated with grass and twigs and there's a see-through visor to protect the eyes – sort of like a cycling helmet which has been customised to look like a tree.

Ria Oh my god.

She starts laughing.

Kurtis *is embarrassed.*

Kurtis It's to protect you on your approach, but whilst keeping the vibe sort of deer-friendly.

Ria *can't stop laughing.*

Kurtis It's quite stupid but I just thought . . . I don't know . . . might help you feel more . . . safe . . .

He's really embarrassed now.

Ria Are you joking!?

KURTIS.

I LOVE IT SO MUCH.

She takes it from him.

Did you make it?

Kurtis (*dead-pan joke*) Is it hard to tell because it looks so professionally done?

Ria *laughs.*

Kurtis Yes, I made it.

Ria *puts it on.*

Kurtis *laughs and smiles – he's really pleased she likes it.*

Kurtis You look great.

Ria I do feel very safe in here actually.

Kurtis I dunno if it'll work . . . but maybe worth a shot to sort your mate out.

Ria *looks at him.*

Ria It's amazing.

Thank you.

She takes the helmet off and places it down somewhere with great care.

Kurtis *is watching her, delighted.*

Ria And I'll definitely try your . . .

She starts doing the exercise – moving her arms slowly, taking slow steps to the side and back – it's very tai chi.

This the vibe?

Kurtis Yeah perfect.

He starts doing it with her – they're in sync opposite each other – **Kurtis** *following* **Ria**'*s lead.*

Ria I am in the shop.

Kurtis I am in the shop.

Ria I am practising the technique.

Kurtis I am practising the technique.

Ria I am looking at Kurtis.

Kurtis I am looking at Ria.

They hold each other's gaze for a moment, both smiling.

Then **Ria** *drops her arms.*

A beat, then:

Ria You know I think Uma is a bit stressed we're hanging out so much.

This comment really hits **Kurtis**, *but he tries to cover it.*

Kurtis Oh really?

Ria Yeah, she keeps being like 'you know you can take it slow'.

It's annoying.

Beat.

Because I really like being around you, Kurtis.

It feels really good.

Beat – **Kurtis** *looks so happy at this.*

Kurtis I really like being around you too.

They kiss – it starts to feel heated – like it's leading to more.

He starts to freak out.

Hang on, wait.

He moves away from her.

Fuck.

Sorry.

Ria No stress.

Kurtis *is breathing heavily, panicked, deciding if he's really going to do what he's about to do.*

Ria Are you ok?

Kurtis Yeah, sorry.

Ria *approaches him.*

Ria There's no pressure, we can just leave that there if you'd rather . . .

Kurtis No, no it's not that, I just . . .

He's freaking out.

Ria Kurtis . . .

She puts a hand on him, comfortingly.

Kurtis *flinches away from her.*

Beat.

Ria Sorry.

Kurtis No I'm sorry.

Fuck.

He stands a distance away from her. He is holding himself strangely. His whole body tense, as if he's about to be hit.

There is a pause – then he makes the choice.

Kurtis I need to tell you something.

Ria Ok.

Kurtis Something you need to know about me before anything happens with us.

Not that it will now, but . . .

If you want to just leave after that's totally ok.

I would just . . .

If you could just let me say my whole bit first before you . . . I would really like that.

Ria Ok . . .

Scene Eleven

Lights up very suddenly on **Glenn***.*

He stands facing the audience.

Glenn I've been at the archives a lot lately.

Preparing for the event.

I've been reading everything I could find on Pemfort.

I wanted everything to be accurate.

And I wanted to find all the stories I could about the Bell Tower. Reasons it was so important to restore.

I found loads on Jane and Frederik, Lady Drongall, Lord Leevage.

And on other owners too. More recent things.

In the 1920s Pemfort was used as the set for loads of films apparently.

And in World War II it sheltered evacuees during the bombings.

Beat.

But then I found this newspaper article from the nineties. Which was different.

Pause.

It was about this woman called Sally Edwards. She had killed herself and her body had been found in the Bell Tower. She'd hung herself from the iron bar.

Only this article was saying the death hadn't immediately been ruled a suicide. The police had been suspicious, because there had been things about the scene which didn't make sense. Unexplained burns on her body. An absence of markings around her neck, indicating that maybe she'd been dead before she'd been hung.

And her husband, Alistair Edwards had initially been taken in for questioning. And everyone in the town thought he'd probably done it. Said he'd always been a nasty man. Known to the police for previous domestic disturbances. That even if he hadn't killed her, he'd certainly driven her to it.

But then eventually, he was just released.

'SALLY EDWARDS DEATH RULED SUICIDE BUT SUSPICIONS LINGER'

'ALISTAIR EDWARDS RELEASED: BUT FEARS REMAIN'

He had been the groundskeeper here when it happened.

They had lived in that little house Uma lives in now.

And there was this photo of him in a fleece with the same logo as mine, looking exactly how you imagine a murderer to look.

And it just made me feel sick.

To think this had been his Pemfort back then.

In the Tower I used to play in with my mum.

And I don't know why I had never heard of it before.

A suicide.

A potential murderer.

The old groundskeeper.

Beat.

Why didn't we know about that story.

Lights down on **Glenn**.

Scene Twelve

Ria *and* **Kurtis**.

A long, awful silence.

Ria I don't know what to say.

Beat.

I thought it was drugs related.

Had wondered if you'd done something violent.

But I imagined some kind of gang . . . I don't know. Not . . .

Beat.

Kurtis I've had all these assessments.

They do all these checks and I'm . . .

They say I'm minimal threat.

Minimal chance of reoffending.

Minimal risk to . . . women.

Ria Jesus.

Beat.

Kurtis Completely rehabilitated.

Beat.

And have been. For years. Every assessment for years, it's the same.

I just really wanted you to know that.

Pause.

And that's how I feel.

I feel like a completely different person.

And I really.

I really understand what I did to her.

How unforgivable it was.

How life-changing it was.

I really understand that.

Pause.

I've done a lot of work on . . . understanding it all.

And honestly sometimes I wonder if it would have been easier if I hadn't.

Because when that moment happens when you fully realise the extent of the damage you've done to someone . . .

Pause.

I thought about killing myself for a long time.

Beat.

I don't know why I'm saying this.

I guess I just . . . I want to show you that I understand.

That I'm sorry.

That all of me is filled with this shame and guilt and I wish every day that I could go back and make it so it didn't happen.

But I can't.

I can just be . . . sorry.

They stare at each other for a long, awful moment.

Blackout.

Scene Thirteen

Ria *and* **Glenn** *sitting in the shop, waiting. The notice board is out.*

Glenn I don't know what to do about food for the event.

Ria (*half somewhere else*) Oh . . . really?

Glenn Yeah. It's just the traditional Pemfort dish in the 1200s, 1600s AND 1700s was this thing called 'Pemfort Pottage', which was a type of porridge made with turnips. So if we want to be historically accurate, we really need to be serving that.

Glenn *looks to* **Ria** *for a reaction, but she doesn't respond, she's somewhere else.*

Glenn But I tried making it last night and it's disgusting.

So I'm worried if we serve that everyone will just leave.

But then we can't exactly have a pizza truck . . .

Can we?

Again **Glenn** *looks at* **Ria** *for a reaction but she doesn't respond.*

Glenn Ria?

Ria Oh . . . sorry.

What was . . .

Glenn Are you ok?

Pause.

Ria I don't know.

Pause.

Glenn She needs to tell him to leave.

Don't you think?

Pause.

Ria I don't know.

I don't know what I think.

A beat.

Then **Uma** *enters.*

All three take each other in for a moment.

Uma Could we talk about it?

Ria (*to* **Glenn**) Maybe a hog roast?

Uma (*an attempt at lightness*) Chickens?

Glenn Please don't do the 'chickens' thing right now.

A painful pause. **Glenn**'s *anger is building.*

(*To* **Uma**.) You need to get rid of him.

He's a bad person.

Uma He's a person.

Who did a bad thing and who is now rehabilitated.

Glenn Something you completely failed to mention on his arrival.

Beat.

Uma I just wanted to give us a chance to see who he was first, without that . . .

Glenn Without the rape conviction 'clouding our judgement'.

Pause.

Uma Well yes, in a way, yes.

Beat.

Kurtis was brought up taught to be violent. He committed a crime. Over ten years ago now. He served his sentence. And he's done the work to change.

And so yes, I think he should be given the chance to not be seen as that person anymore.

A pause.

And it makes them . . .

It's the statistics, the men who integrate, manage to join a community. Those are the ones that don't reoffend.

Beat.

And I just thought if anywhere could take on someone like that. Maybe it could be us.

Pause – rage is building in **Glenn**.

Glenn This is all so fucked up.

I feel like we're in a true crime documentary.

Is that why you like it? Is this all really exciting to you? Hearing all this fucked up stuff?

Ria Glenn.

Glenn (*to* **Uma**) How do you even know that? About the statistics? Been googling all about it have you?

Beat.

Uma Yes, I have.

It was a decision for me too you know. Bringing him here.

Glenn A decision which wasn't just yours to make.

We aren't part of your little social experiment, we had a right to know who he was.

You've put Ria's safety at risk.

Uma I haven't.

He's completely safe. I would bet my life on it.

Beat.

But listen, Glenn, I know sometimes it's hard to see the complexity of it all and /

This comment suddenly makes **Glenn** *furious – he's shaking with the anger of it.*

Glenn / No don't you dare.

No way.

Don't you dare tell me that just because I think the way I think I don't understand. 'Oh little Glenn, he just doesn't quite understand the nuance of it all. Glenn's a bit "on the spectrum" isn't he, Glenn's a bit "not getting it"'.

You just have no idea what you're talking about, and you think you get it but you just really, really don't.

Men like that don't change.

They just do a good job of hiding it for a bit.

And you're trying so hard to make it complicated, but it isn't.

He's just a bad person.

And he'll have that inside of him, sitting in there, waiting until the day Ria tries to break it off with him, or he doesn't get something else he thinks he's entitled to.

And then you watch it all spill back out.

A long pause – **Uma** *knows what* **Glenn** *is referring to here and it softens her response, but she's still strong in her conviction.*

Uma I'm not kicking him out, Glenn.

I'm sorry.

Kurtis *enters.*

A pause – nobody sure what to do.

Uma Right. Shall we get started?

Glenn?

Glenn *stands, trying to decide if he's going to stay or leave.*

A horrible moment. Everyone waiting.

Then eventually, **Glenn** *moves over to the board.*

A beat.

Glenn 'The Death of Sally Edwards'.

I think we have to include it.

Uma How would we include it?

Beat.

Glenn I don't know.

Obviously, a re-enactment would be in very poor taste . . .

Uma Do you not think it might be best to just leave it out? It's such a sad and horrible story.

Ria I dunno, the Ghost of Lady Drongall is a horrible story if you think about it.

Married off to a man twice her age. And then attacked by his insane manservant. Dragged down into the dungeons to die whilst a party for the wedding she never wanted happened above her.

Beat.

I mean come to think of it they're all pretty horrible.

All these 'fun stories of the castle'. It's all just violence and desperation.

And now we're going to act it out like it's all so fun.

Glenn That's true.

Maybe we shouldn't be doing any of them.

Uma I don't think that's true, Glenn.

Nobody is saying what happened in these stories is great, but it was a very long time ago, and I think that does make a difference to how we speak about them.

There are people in the village who will have known Alistair and Sally Edwards. So maybe that's why it doesn't feel like history just yet.

Pause.

Glenn Why does nobody talk about it?

Uma They do talk about it.

Or they did. When I first moved to Pemfort people would talk about it a lot in fact. How awful it was, how they thought he'd almost definitely done it.

But then I guess as time moves on . . . People move on.

Glenn And then everyone kept it secret?

Uma It's not secret, Glenn.

If you ask Pete or Sue or anyone, I'm sure they'd tell you about it.

But it was just a horrible thing which happened, what's more to say about it really.

People don't 'not talk about it'. They just don't talk about it.

It's not . . . relevant anymore.

Beat – **Glenn** *is considering.*

Glenn I think we should do an information board.

We can put it by the Tower.

It doesn't have to be a huge thing. But I don't think we should just let it be forgotten.

What happened to her isn't irrelevant.

Beat.

Kurtis Should we maybe also add it to the timeline?

A horribly awkward pause here.

Glenn *looks at* **Ria**.

Glenn (*to* **Ria**) I guess maybe you could do that?

Seeing as you worked on it.

Uma Well I guess Ria and Kurtis can do that together.

This comment gets to **Glenn**.

Glenn I just worry if that's *wise*.

This comment gets to **Kurtis**.

Kurtis (*getting upset*) I'm not going / to . . .

Glenn *and* **Uma** *both ignore* **Kurtis** *and continue.*

Uma There is no reason the two of them can't do it together just like before.

Glenn There is definitely a *reason* / the two of them can't do it just like before.

Ria / Glenn . . .

Kurtis / Or I can just do it by myself, or Ria / can I wasn't suggesting . . .

Again, they ignore him. The frustration is becoming overwhelming.

Glenn / We need to ensure that Ria is *safe*.

In one sudden movement of frustration **Kurtis** *swipes at a glass object near him and it smashes onto the floor.*

Kurtis (*as he does it*) I AM SAFE.

A horrible moment – **Glenn**, **Ria** *and* **Uma** *all turn to stare at him.*

Kurtis *is completely overcome with the frustration of it all, and then in turn the horrible realisation of what he's just done.*

Kurtis Fuck.

I'm sorry.

Beat.

I'm sorry.

He looks broken. He bends down as if he's going to try and pick up the glass but ends up half collapsing onto the floor instead.

The other three stand, looking down at him. He looks so desperate and hopeless in this moment.

Then after a long pause **Ria** *moves over to him and starts to clear up the broken glass.*

As she's doing this, **Uma** *asks:*

Uma Ria, do you feel safe doing the timeline with Kurtis?

Beat – **Ria** *answers whilst looking at* **Kurtis**.

Ria Yeah.

Yes.

I do.

Scene Fourteen

Kurtis *alone in the shop, both practise and real swords are out. He's been waiting.*

Then **Glenn** *enters.*

They take each other in for a moment.

Kurtis I didn't know if you were going to come.

Glenn Well we need to get it practised before the event don't we.

Pause.

Right.

Shall we do a slow once-through?

Kurtis Sure.

Glenn *and* **Kurtis** *both pick up a practise sword.*

They stand opposite each other.

Then they begin their routine.

They go through it once slowly, not speaking, it's come on a lot since we last saw it – it's smooth and well-practised.

Glenn Great.

That was good.

Ok.

Shall we do an 'as if on the day' one?

Kurtis Sure.

They both put down their wooden sword and pick up a real one.

They stand opposite each other again.

They repeat the routine with the real swords, but this time it feels like **Glenn** *really goes for* **Kurtis** *– there is real anger in his actions, maybe he's actually out to hurt him?* **Kurtis** *seems alarmed – he defends himself, as part of the routine but also maybe partly for real?*

They end in their rehearsed position – **Glenn** *pinning* **Kurtis**. **Glenn** *holds here, looking straight into* **Kurtis***'s eyes. Anger boiling in him.*

A pause.

And then **Glenn** *relaxes, freeing* **Kurtis** *from his position.*

Glenn *puts his sword down.*

Kurtis *puts his down too.*

They look at each other for a moment, **Glenn** *almost willing* **Kurtis** *to say something.* **Kurtis** *doesn't.*

Glenn My dad used to hit my mum you know.

Beat.

Kurtis I'm so sorry, Glenn, that's horrible.

Glenn It's partly why she is how she is. Because of him.

He messed with her head too much.

Pause – **Kurtis** *doesn't know what to say.*

Kurtis That's awful /

Glenn / Each time he'd do it; it would be a little bit worse.

And then each time he'd be even more sorry.

Promise even more he'd never do it again.

And sometimes he'd last quite a long time.

But he never stopped.

Pause.

He's been gone for years now but I don't think she'll ever get better. She was just too afraid for too long, it's like she can't shake it now.

And the worst bit is sometimes I really hate her for it. For being so unwell.

Which is horrible.

Because it's not her fault. I know it's not her fault.

Pause.

But I know that type of anger.

Where you think you could really hurt someone.

Where you sort of want to hurt someone, because everything feels so unfair.

They look at each other for a moment.

Glenn But I'd never do it.

Kurtis *doesn't know what to say.*

Kurtis I'm not for a moment excusing what I did you know.

Glenn I'm just saying.

I think I've had that feeling, that you must have had.

I come from a 'violent troubled home'.

But I would never *choose* to hurt someone the way you did.

Scene Fifteen

Ria *alone in the shop.*

Kurtis *enters.*

Ria Hey.

Kurtis Hey.

Pause – then **Ria** *sort of half-laughs weirdly.*

Ria Well this is awkward.

Kurtis I can just go, leave you to it, if that's easier.

Ria Ah no, it's alright.

Pause.

Shouldn't take long anyway.

Beat.

Ok. So. Glenn has sent me some very clear instructions.

Reading off her phone.

No images. Clear simple language outlining the incident . . .

Oh right, he's also sent me the exact text he wants.

Kurtis *is looking at the timeline.*

Kurtis I guess maybe we can make an arrow and put it above?

Ria Yeah, sounds good.

Kurtis *moves towards* **Ria** *to get the things he needs.* **Ria** *fractionally stiffens and moves fractionally away from him. It's subtle, but he notices, and it causes him pain.*

Then he continues getting the stuff, and politely moves away from **Ria**, *keeping distance.*

There is a pause. **Ria** *stands, unsure what to do with herself.*

Ria I wanted to tell you it . . . er . . . it totally worked by the way.

She's smiling at him – he looks confused.

With the deer. The breathing and the helmet and everything.

I did it.

A beat – **Kurtis** *suddenly forgets it's awkward – his whole manner changes in the face of this excellent news.*

Kurtis You're joking!?

Ria *laughs – and their old ease with each other is suddenly back.*

Ria I'm not.

I felt like a *complete* mad woman, and it was VERY SCARY but I have successfully FREED THE DEER.

Kurtis Oh my god! RIA. You *COMPLETE LEGEND.*

That's so . . .!

We can sense him really wanting to hug **Ria** *here – but he doesn't. She senses it too and it mutes the moment slightly.*

Kurtis That's so good.

Beat.

And it didn't go for you or anything?

Ria No, not at all. It was actually so smooth.

A pause.

Kurtis Well come on then, give me the low-down.

She laughs.

Ria Well I had obviously been wearing the helmet every time I went into the garden, so he got acclimatised to my new look.

Kurtis Obviously.

Ria So then one day after a while of that I saw him and . . . I don't know, he seemed really chill that day or something and it just . . . felt like the right moment.

So I started moving towards him like SUPER slowly – and at first I felt myself getting a bit freaked out, but I just kept breathing really slow and trying to focus on like 'my foot is touching the grass, I can hear a bird . . .' and all that. And I could feel myself getting calmer. And I got right up close to him. But he didn't run, he just stood there with his head to one side like 'what the hell is she doing'.

And we stood there next to each other for a moment. Breathing.

And then super slowly I started to raise my hand to his antler. And when I finally put my fingers on the wire it was like – something in the air suddenly changed. Like he understood what I was trying to do. And I just knew he wasn't going to hurt me.

And he just stood there, perfectly still, as I unwound it.

And then I stepped back. And we looked at each other for a moment. And then he left.

And it was . . . it was sort of totally incredible to be honest.

It felt like this huge . . . I don't know.

Moment.

They're looking at each other – both of them eyes bright.

Kurtis That's incredible.

God, Ria. You're . . .

He wants to tell **Ria** *she's incredible. Maybe in this moment he's realising he loves her a bit. And maybe she sees that in him too.*

A beat – nobody sure what to do.

Then he breaks it.

Kurtis Have you seen him since?

Ria Nah.

I hope we're still pals.

Kurtis I'm *sure.* I bet he'll be round soon, and he'll bring you a pinecone or something to say thanks.

Ria *laughs.*

Ria Imagine if he shows up in a helmet and starts inching towards me to try and take my jacket off me or something.

Kurtis And doing a little breathing exercise.

They both laugh, then smile at each other for a moment.

Then suddenly it's like they both remember it's weird.

A shift in tone.

Kurtis What was the wording Glenn wanted on this?

Ria Er . . . let me get it, one sec.

She gets out her phone. Then . . .

(*Reading slowly as* **Kurtis** *writes.*) Ok, it's '1998 – The body of Sally Edwards is found in the Bell Tower. Her husband,

Alistair Edwards, is arrested for murder, but her death is later ruled suicide'.

Kurtis *writes this on his board.*

Kurtis Ok.

Done.

There is a pause – both unsure what to do now.

Kurtis Hey I wanted to . . .

Ria *uncomfortable.*

Kurtis I just wanted to give you something.

Kurtis *moves slowly to his bag, retrieves some papers – hands them out to* **Ria** *momentarily, then thinks better of it and places them on the counter.*

Kurtis It's my psychological assessments. All of them, since I got out.

Just if you wanted to see them. They're there.

She doesn't know what to say. He continues, he's obviously semi-prepared this.

And I wanted to say that if you wanted to ask me anything about my conviction, just . . . if it would be helpful to know anything . . . you can ask me anything you want.

He can't look at her.

Ria Er . . . ok.

Kurtis Obviously you don't have to, and I know you said you were just going to take some time and obviously I totally get that and won't message you or anything, obviously, but just saying that . . .

In case there was anything . . .

He is uncomfortable, he starts to pack up his stuff.

Anyway, maybe I'll /

Ria / Did you plead guilty?

A pause.

I guess that's something I've been wondering.

Beat.

Kurtis Er, yeah. I did.

A pause – he hesitates, then explains:

The evidence was undeniable because they had CCTV footage, so I was advised to plead guilty.

Ria (*disappointed by this explanation*) Oh, right.

Kurtis And also I was guilty. And I should have faced the consequences of that.

But it took a while you know, to feel like that.

It wasn't.

It wasn't an overnight thing.

Pause.

Ria Did you ever talk to her afterwards?

Kurtis I sent her a letter.

I don't know if she ever got it.

I think she did.

Beat.

I really hope she did.

Pause.

Listen, whatever you need me to do or whatever you need to see to feel . . . just let me know.

He hesitates, this next bit is hard to say . . .

And if you did want me to leave, I would.

Close to tears thinking about it.

But I would really love to stay.

A pause – **Ria** *doesn't respond to this, but we can tell it's hit her.*

Then **Kurtis** *holds out the sign he's made for Sally Edwards.*

Kurtis Here.

Ria *takes the sign off him.*

He starts to leave.

Kurtis I'll see you tomorrow. So weird that it's finally here.

Ria Yeah, I know.

Beat.

See you tomorrow.

Kurtis *exits.*

Ria *attaches the extra sign to the timeline.*

There is a pause.

Uma *enters.*

Uma Hello chicken.

Ria Hi.

Pause.

Uma How did that go then?

Ria Yeah, fine.

Bit weird.

The vibe is weird between them.

Uma Are you very angry at me?

Ria I don't know.

I'm not not angry.

Beat.

I still don't really understand why you did it. Like gave him the job and everything.

You don't know him.

Uma I do know him.

Ria Yeah but not like really. Not like how you know me and Glenn.

Uma No, not like you and Glenn.

Beat.

But I do feel like I understand him very much on some level.

Pause.

I know it's not at all the same, but the things I put Harry and his father through when I was using.

I guess I know how it feels to be so ashamed about who you once were. To spend all your time replaying events in your mind, screaming at this younger version of yourself to make a different decision.

And I don't know what would have happened to me if it wasn't for Pemfort back then. It gave me the opportunity to become a new version of myself.

And I guess I just wanted to give that to Kurtis.

Beat.

He was so alone.

And it changes everything. That feeling of belonging somewhere.

Beat.

Ria I just don't know if he does belong here.

I thought he did.

But this all just feels so . . . not Pemfort.

Uma I think that's why it's the perfect place for him.

Beat.

An actual second chance for someone like Kurtis doesn't just mean sitting in a corner being sombre and remorseful for the rest of his life.

It means being allowed to be silly, to have a laugh, to get involved in somewhere like this.

It means being allowed to *live.*

Pause – **Ria** *doesn't know what to say, she's taking it all in.*

Uma Right. I'm going to do one final check on everything and then straight to bed for everyone I reckon!

I can't believe it's tomorrow.

So exciting hey.

Ria Yeah.

So exciting.

She takes the assessment documents **Kurtis** *has left on the side as she leaves.*

Scene Sixteen

Music begins, quiet at first but getting louder.

Glenn*'s voice on the tannoy.*

Glenn *(off)* Hello everyone! Listen to me now please I'm doing an announcement.

Beat – **Glenn** *changes into his 'announcement voice'.*

Thank you for coming to Pemfort's FIRST Living History event.

The opening remarks will soon take place in the armoury, please make your way over there to begin . . . your adventure.

Candlelight flickers. We are in the armoury. It's genuinely quite dark and atmospheric. We think for a moment that perhaps we actually have stepped back in time.

Glenn *enters dressed as Frederik; he wears a huge cape which conceals his sword. He makes his way to the centre of the stage. He stands close to the audience.*

He looks out at everyone for a moment.

Glenn Welcome dear friends . . . to Pemfort.

We stand here today, on our history.

We often think our history is buried deep. Dusty and forgotten.

When in reality it's lying just below our feet.

Laying the foundations of everything.

For what we do in the present is only ever dictated by our past. And we can only really understand where we are now, by understanding what has come before.

Beat.

And so, I congratulate you the people of Pemfort, for coming here today to be part of Pemfort's very first Living History event!

Pemfort is a place which has been very many different things to very many different people.

It has been a place of great triumphs and victories. And a place of great pain and suffering.

We come here today to acknowledge all of it.

To shine a light on Pemfort's treasures. And on its skeletons.

For it is only by seeing how our timeline has moved us through all of it – from hardship to prosperity, from pain to joy, from war to peace . . .

That we can recognise the biggest lesson that history teaches us.

We must be ready for change.

There is a change in tone here, **Glenn**'s *opening speech is now transitioning into the battle scene . . .*

And with that allow me to introduce myself!

For my name is Frederik de Bisschop and I am heir to Pemfort.

But the times are not what they once were. Our beautiful life here has been disrupted.

Evil has entered our lands.

And we are under attack.

Suddenly **Kurtis** *appears, dressed as the evil bishop, sword drawn.*

Kurtis Stand back, little boy!

This is my castle now.

Glenn *draws his sword quick as a flash and turns to face* **Kurtis**.

Glenn It's potentially a fort actually, you ignorant evil bishop.

And you have no right to it!

He charges at **Kurtis**.

The fight is great and very dramatic.

There is one slight wobble in the routine, where **Glenn** *lunges and misses* **Kurtis**, *which is not as it should happen.* **Glenn** *panics at the error, but* **Kurtis** *quickly moves to the side and motions for* **Glenn** *to lunge again. This time they pull the sequence off and as* **Glenn** *lunges,* **Kurtis** *spins and traps him.*

Kurtis This is for England!

He goes for **Glenn***, but in a beautifully rehearsed moment* **Glenn** *escapes at the last moment and corners* **Kurtis** *in return.*

Glenn *stands over* **Kurtis***, sword at his heart.*

Glenn And THIS! Is for PEMFORTTTTTTTTT!!!!

Glenn *fake stabs* **Kurtis** *in the heart very dramatically.*

Kurtis *dies dramatically.*

Glenn *is victorious dramatically.*

It's all excellent.

There is a dramatic pause and then the mood suddenly switches to one of festivity.

Glenn *and* **Kurtis** *get up and bow.*

Glenn Thank you everyone!!

That was the infamous Battle of the Bishops!

You can now enjoy the medicinal herb gardens in the outhouses, hear the outrageous scandals of Lord Leevage in the red room quarters, or wax dip your own candle with Big Dog Pete in the turret. But whatever you do . . . don't go down into the dungeons . . . they're haunted.

Please enjoy the rest of your day and don't litter or I will actually kill you with this sword just like how I killed the evil bishop.

Uma *and* **Ria** *enter from where they have been watching the fight – both clapping enthusiastically.*

Uma So good! So bloody good you absolute superstars!

She hugs both of them in turn.

Glenn *grins at* **Kurtis***, excited, more boyish than we've seen him before.*

Glenn (*to* **Kurtis**) That was good, wasn't it!?

Kurtis I'd say so yeah!

Glenn Thank you. For helping . . . when I . . .

Kurtis Of course.

A beat – they smile at each other.

Glenn Oh my god, I'm excited!!

We are off to an excellent start!

I'm going to go check on the food trucks.

He starts to exit.

Uma come on!

Uma *rushes after him.*

Uma Coming Glennychicken!

Kurtis *and* **Ria** *alone.*

A beat.

Ria Great job.

Kurtis Thanks.

He starts to pull off his costume a bit.

Do you think people saw the little double take?

Ria No, not at all.

You smashed it.

Kurtis *smiles.* **Ria** *doesn't.*

A beat.

Kurtis I was going to go and watch Sue's haunting, if you wanted to . . .

Pause, **Ria** *is hesitating, unsure if she's really about to do what she's about to do.*

Kurtis *feels something is wrong. His smile suddenly drops. He stands very still. He waits for it.*

Then eventually . . .

Ria I don't think you can stay here, Kurtis.

Pause.

I've been turning it over and over in my mind.

Willing myself to be ok with it.

Pause.

I read your assessments.

There's this early one. Where they talk about how you felt looking at the evidence of the attack.

How you felt looking at these photos of her . . . after . . .

Beat.

And then I watched you do that sword fight. With *Glenn*. In *Pemfort*.

Pause.

And I just can't . . . I can't be ok with you being here.

Kurtis*'s eyes are filling with tears.*

Kurtis I really am who I am right now you know.

Ria You are.

And you are also the person who beat and raped a woman.

I can't look at you and not see it.

Kurtis I'm not asking you to not see it.

Ria But I can't move past it.

It's too big.

Pause.

And I can feel it . . . getting inside of everything.

Kurtis *starts to break down.*

Kurtis You said before you felt safe around me.

Ria I don't think it's about being safe.

I think it's about the fact you ever did it in the first place.

Pause.

Part of me wishes you'd just never told me.

Pause.

Kurtis Please, Ria. This is the closest I've ever got to being let back in.

And I don't know if I can do another seven years like that again.

Ria Maybe the next place you try will be better.

Kurtis You know that's not true.

There is a long pause as **Ria** *looks at him.*

Kurtis I don't know what the point in it all was.

Of sitting with Kev in that little room for hours and hours and hours. Understanding exactly why I was a complete piece of shit, exactly the series of events which lead to me being a complete piece of shit, carefully figuring out how I would never be a complete piece of shit again.

What was the point in all of that. If this is what happens now.

Pause.

What am I meant to do now, with all these years I have left.

Pause.

Ria I'm sorry.

I really hope you find a place where you can be.

Pause.

Because I really do / [love you]

Kurtis / Please don't say it.

Pause.

Ria But it can't be here.

Kurtis *is completely broken. He suddenly seems incredibly weak; he steadies himself.*

He exits.

Ria *remains where she is.*

A moment passes.

Glenn *and* **Uma** *enter.*

Glenn Where is he?

Ria Gone.

The three stand together for a moment.

Blackout.

End.

www.ingramcontent.com/pod-product-compliance
Lightning Source LLC
LaVergne TN
LVHW052342100826
845147LV00021B/1160

* 9 7 8 1 3 5 0 6 4 3 5 9 8 *